POTS, PANS, AND PASSPORTS

POTS, PANS, AND PASSPORTS

RECIPES TO TAKE YOU AROUND THE WORLD

NINA ZIPPAY

A RADICAL COOKS PRODUCTION

Copyright © 2022
By Nina Zippay

All Rights Reserved

Published in the United States by Radical Cooks.

www.potspansanspassports.com
www.radicalcooks.com

Radical Cooks is a registered trademark of Radical Radishes LLC.

Identifiers:

ISBN: 979-8-88759-294-7 (paperback)
ISBN: 979-8-88759-171-1 (hardcover)
ISBN: 979-8-88759-172-8 (ebook)

Subjects: Cooking, Travel, Geography

Cover Photography by Paul Andresen
Book Photography by Paul Andresen

First Edition

Other books by the author coming soon:

A Taste of California History
Seasonal Eats, Seasonal Harmony
The Outdoor Kitchen

This book is dedicated to my mother,
Louise Betty DeRe Zippay.

CONTENTS

Exploring The World Through The Kitchen Door Ix
How To Use This Book xi

CHAPTER 1: AFRICA 1

ETHIOPIA 3
   Kik Alicha 5
   Injera 7

EGYPT 9
   Koshari 11
   Om Ali 13

MOROCCO 15
   Couscous 16
   Moroccan Spice Blend 17
   Moroccan Vegetable Stew 19

CHAPTER 2: EUROPE 21

ITALY 23
   Potato Gnocchi 25
   Pesto Sauce 26
   Italian Wedding Cookies 27

GREECE 29
   Greek Salad 31
   Zucchini Fritters 32

FRANCE 35
   My Favorite Crepes 37

IRELAND 39
   Colcannon 41

CHAPTER 3: ASIA 43

JAPAN 45
   Simple Sushi Nori Maki 46
   Sushi Rice 47
   Okonomiyaki 48

CHINA 51
   Stir Fry 52

VIETNAM 55
   Vietnamese Spring Or "Summer" Rolls.. 56

INDIA 59
   Cauliflower & Pea Curry... 60
   Nan or Naan Bread 61
   Curry Spice Blend.. 63

THAILAND 65
   Green Papaya Salad (Som Tum)... 67
   Sticky Rice with Mango 69

CHAPTER 4: AUSTRALIA 71

AUSTRALIA ~ THE COUNTRY 73
   Anzac Biscuits 75
   Vegemite Sandwich 77

NEW ZEALAND 79
   Pavlova 81

CHAPTER 5: NORTH AMERICA 83

CUBA 85
   Moros y Cristianos ~ Black Beans & Rice.. 86
   Fried plantains.. 87

MEXICO 89
   Homemade Tortillas 90
   Tostadas 93

UNITED STATES OF AMERICA 95
   Key Lime Pie 97
   S'mores 99

CHAPTER 6: SOUTH AMERICA 101

BRAZIL 103
   Brigadeiros 105

ARGENTINA 107
   Empanadas 108
   Alfajores 110

PERU 113
   Traditional Peruvian Ceviche.. 114
   Veggie Ceviche.. 115

CHAPTER 7: ANTARCTICA 117

   Sledging Biscuits... 119

Acknowledgments... 121

Resources 123

Cooking Conversion Chart 125

About the Author 127

EXPLORING THE WORLD THROUGH THE KITCHEN DOOR

Each year the holiday season started off with my mom asking "Where should we go for Christmas?" "Greece? Italy? Mexico" I'd reply. For each Christmas as a child, I traveled to a different country. One year my family went to Sweden. Another year we traveled to Mexico, then Italy, and the next year, Greece. Even though I grew up in a small town (population 200!) I learned so much about the world from these adventures.

In full disclosure, we never actually physically went to Mexico, Greece, Sweden, or Italy. I never traveled the world until I was an adult. What we did do was sit down at our kitchen table, pour over cookbooks borrowed from the local library, select a country, and design a feast. My mother and I would make dishes found in these cookbooks to serve at Christmas to friends and family. It was not easy. If we were going to Greece we would have to call around and find specialty grocery stores in the bigger cities near us asking if they sold grape leaves. If we were going to Italy we'd scour the back pages of fancy cooking magazines like Bon Appetit for frozen squid with the hopes they could ship in time for the holidays.

Over the years I learned how to make dolmades (Greece), tortillas (Mexico), and pickled herring (Sweden). On Christmas Eve we'd clear off the table and set out a feast. Friends and family would arrive and look suspiciously at the squid swimming in red sauce. Other times they would dive into Mexican tamales. Some were willing to try it; others would stick up their noses and call us crazy or weird. We paid no attention to the latter. Somewhere, deep inside my heart, I knew the real fun was found in the discovery of new countries and cuisine.

My mother barely went to high school and had only traveled from her birthplace of Chicago, Illinois to our central Illinois town of 200 people. Yet, she created a learning institution to rival most culinary schools with her curiosity, tenacity, and open-mindedness. This book is for her. It is also for you and your future generations. I hope this cookbook inspires you to travel and explore the world and appreciate its culinary wonders in whatever shape you choose. And I hope you pass along the tradition.

~Nina Zippay

HOW TO USE THIS BOOK

A cookbook is a perfect way to always be learning and to keep your mind fresh and active. No matter your age, you can use this book to learn new recipes and learn about the world. Let it be the inspiration to launch your next travel adventure. Create a feast featuring a particular country, like my mom and I did, for friends and family in your own kitchen. Or use this book to liven up the weekly meal plan. Consider it an invitation to take one of our cooking classes, virtually or in person.

SAME SAME, ONLY DIFFERENT

When my husband and I traveled throughout Southeast Asia we often heard the phrase "same, same, only different." The phrase was applied in many contexts, from buying counterfeit goods to trying local dishes. As you peruse this book, you might find it remarkable that rice is ubiquitous, yet "different" depending upon how it is made and where it is served. Check out our recipe from Cuba, Moros y Cristianos, and see how the rice is used there, then contrast it with our version of fried rice on our website. How are the recipes similar? How are they different? And why? For a more in-depth "rice talk," see our blog at our website **Pots, Pans, and Passports**. Then extrapolate, asking yourself, "Are we the same? Are we different? And how?"

FOR KIDS, YOUNG AND NOT-SO-YOUNG

I created the class series, called **Pots, Pans, and Passports** to help students expand their knowledge of the world via cooking. In class, students learn to make different dishes from different countries. In addition to bringing broader global awareness to our students, thereby boosting cultural intelligence, **Pots, Pans, and Passports** does so much more. In general, I have found that cooking enhances the following skill sets:

Math ~ counting, weighing, and measuring
Language Arts ~ sequencing, following directions
Teamwork and collaboration ~ students develop social skills by working together and communicating in groups, communicating with peers, and asking relevant questions

If you are part of a family, or if you are teaching as a parent or otherwise, you can use this book to teach any of the above-referenced skills while teaching broader based concepts such as cultural intelligence, diversity, and more. We have more resources and ideas to be found on our website. Check it out!

PANTRY NOTES AND COOKING TIPS

I created this book and my classes in the United States, so the measurements and temperatures use imperial measurements (cups, tablespoons, and teaspoons) and fahrenheit instead of celsius. There is a conversion chart in the back of the book to use if you are based in a country which uses the metric system.

This cookbook is mostly vegetarian, as am I. Our classes are the same, as I found it to be the more inclusive way to welcome as many people as possible to the table. Eating more vegetables and less meat is not only good for you but it is also good for the planet. I hope these recipes will inspire to you to eat less meat. If you want to adapt some of the recipes using meat, such as the stir fry, this is always an option.

Many recipes include substitutions for specialty ingredients (e.g., palm sugar, caster sugar, etc.) but there are some recipes in which ingredients might not readily be available in all regions of the world. Some specialty items can be purchased via our website or online. Other fresh ingredients such as a green papaya may be a little more difficult to find.

I don't like to make people buy a lot of things for one recipe but not be able to use them on a regular basis. Starting with the basics, here are some kitchen tools which you will need for most recipes in this book. Other specialty items, such as gnocchi paddles, woks, and tagines are optional.

KITCHEN TOOLS AND EQUIPMENT

DUTCH OVEN OR STOCK POT: Either will suffice for stews and soups.

FOOD PROCESSOR: I have a food processor and use it on a regular basis for sauces (NOT chimichurri), and more.

KNIVES YOU NEED ~ CHEF KNIFE, PARING KNIFE, AND SERRATED BREAD KNIFE: These are the three knives to have in the kitchen.

MANDOLINE: I didn't have one of these in the early years of my cooking adventures and now that I do, it makes shredding cabbage, slicing cucumbers, potatoes, and more so much easier. The blade is VERY sharp so please exercise caution while using. Go slow.

MIXER: a stand mixer or hand mixer will help make your meringues and allow you to quickly create the batter for cookies and crepes.

PARCHMENT PAPER: I do a LOT of dishes so parchment paper makes the cleaning process go a lot faster.

RICE MAKER: A good rice maker will expedite the cooking process and allow you freedom to prep while the rice is cooking. It also works great with other grains, too.

SHEET PANS: baking sheet pans, preferably rimmed, will be an essential tool for roasting veggies, baking cookies, and general kitchen prep.

SKILLET: I love a good cast iron skillet or a thick bottom skillet.

WHISK: Not only are they fun to use, whisks add air into mixtures and help better blend ingredients.

COOKING TIPS

COOKING IS A PROCESS. Recipes rarely tell the full story or go into detail about technique. There is trial and error and eventually trial and success. This is the cooking process. I did include notes for recipes where I thought a little more explanation was needed.

READ. MEASURE. READ AGAIN. I often give this instruction to my students. I even follow my own instructions once in a while. I find when I don't read the recipe a few times I forget a step and end up with a big mess.

MISE OUT. Another essential step is "mise en place." It is a term in French which translates into the idea that you pull your ingredients, measure, chop, slice, and grate before you start cooking. You also have the opportunity to create a beautiful display in the kitchen. When I make a stir fry, I love to set out all my veggies, chop and slice and mince and artfully lay them out on a plate or platter. It makes the cooking process meditative and fun.

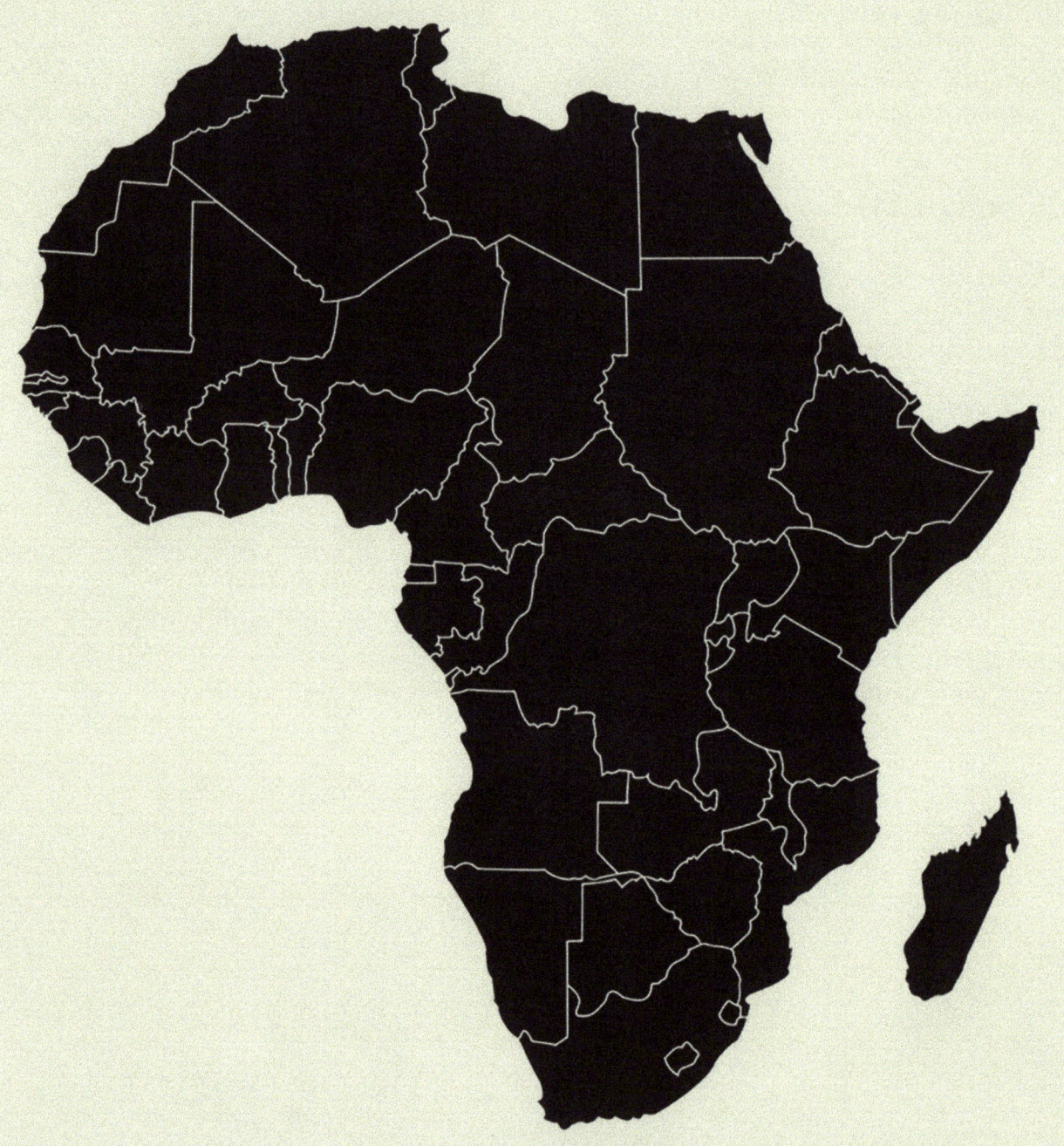

AFRICA

When we think of Africa we often imagine wild animals, such as lions, elephants, and giraffes. But Africa is so much more! First, it's huge! So big that it is the world's second-largest continent. Second, there are a lot of people. It's the second-most-populous continent. Third, the countries in Africa can be very different in terms of food and culture. What people eat in Egypt, a country to the north is very different from what people eat in Ethiopia, a country situated to the east. One of the reasons for the different types of food is that there are so many different climates in Africa. The types of plants and animals living and growing in the deserts of Africa will be different from those grown in the jungles or grasslands. Because of the different climates, people will eat different things. In this chapter, we will take a look at three countries in Africa ~ Ethiopia, Egypt, and Morocco.

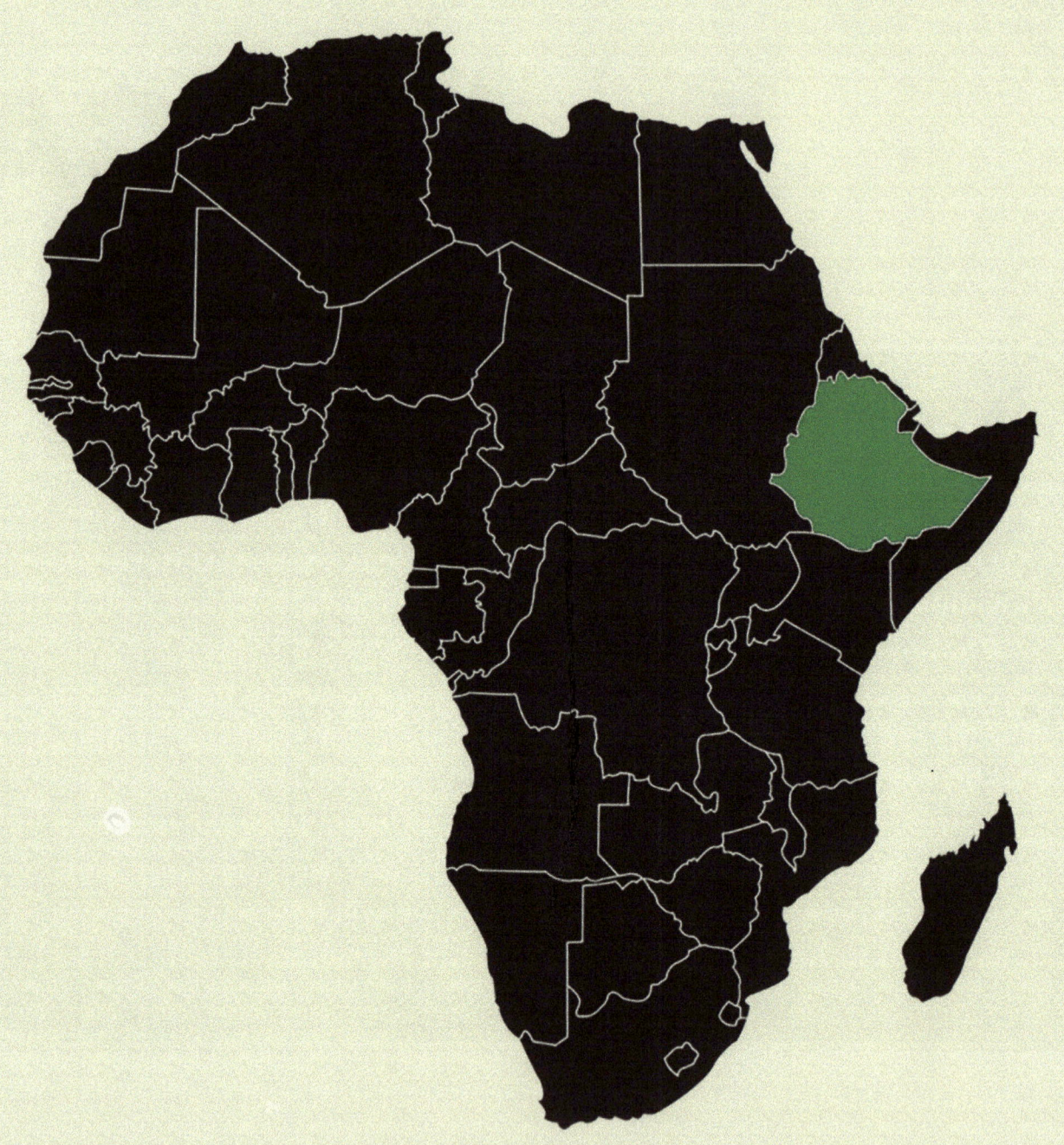

ETHIOPIA

Ethiopia is located in eastern Africa and has mountains, and deserts, and lies next to the Red Sea. It fell under colonial rule just once, from 1935 to 1946, when Italy invaded and attempted to colonize it. Other than that time period, Ethiopia was and has been an independent country.

Do you like spicy foods? Then you'll *love* Ethiopian food! Berbere (bare-BARE-ee) is a traditional spicy paste that Ethiopians have used to preserve and flavor foods. It's made of chili peppers, garlic, ginger, basil, fenugreek, and korarima (a spice grown in Ethiopia).

If you want something a little milder, then try Kik Alicha. If you are feeling really adventurous, try making some injera to serve with it. Or if you are able, find an Ethiopian restaurant in your area and buy the injera pre-made. Be sure to sit down and order two or three dishes before you go, too.

Kik Alicha
(ETHIOPIAN YELLOW SPLIT PEA STEW)
{serves 4 to 6 easily}

Kik Alicha, a slightly less spicy stew, is usually made with yellow lentils or split peas. It is a dish we frequently make in our classes. Not only it is full of protein, it can be flavored to your liking, and everyone loves to eat it with injera.

- 4 small purple onions
- 4 cloves garlic, coarsely minced
- 1 cup olive oil
- 1 16-ounce bag of yellow split peas or yellow lentils
- 2 teaspoons turmeric, powdered, or 2 tablespoons, freshly grated turmeric
- salt, and pepper, to taste

In a large, heavy pot, cover peas with water. Bring the peas to a boil and then reduce heat to medium-low and cook until the peas are tender. This should take about 30-45 minutes. Peel the onions and either puree them in a food processor or blender or finely mince. Saute the onions in a heavy pot until they are just turning brown. Add the olive oil, turmeric, and garlic and stir. Partially drain the peas but reserve some of the water they were cooked in, about two cups, in a bowl. Add the cooked split peas (water included) to the onion mixture. Simmer on low heat until the peas are consistent with or similar to pea soup. If it becomes dry, add back in some of the reserved water. Salt to taste. Serve with injera.

Injera
~ the edible tablecloth ~
{serves 4–6}

It's a tablecloth. It's an eating utensil. It's food. How can one thing be all three? Grab some injera and find out. *Injera*, a spongy, sour flatbread used throughout Ethiopia to scoop up meat and vegetable stews, lines the tray on which the thick stews and other dishes are served, soaking up their juices as the meal progresses. When this injera is gone, the meal is done.

Injera is made with *teff*, a tiny, round grain that grows in the mountains of Ethiopia. Making injera is a time-consuming process so for our classes we often will go to an Ethiopian restaurant or grocery store to buy it ready made. If you don't have any local Ethiopian restaurants in your area then you can order some online from any of the websites listed in our Resources section on our website. Or you can try making it yourself with the following recipe.

1/4 cup teff flour
3/4 cup all-purpose flour
1 cup water
a pinch of salt
vegetable oil

Sift together the teff flour and all-purpose flour into a medium-sized bowl. Whisk in the water doing your best to reduce lumps. Cover the bowl tightly with either plastic wrap or a tight lid and allow the batter to ferment for one to three days. The batter should start to bubble and become "sour" or tangy in taste. Stir in the salt. Heat a nonstick pan or lightly oiled cast-iron skillet, making sure the surface of the pan is very hot before adding batter. Pour a thin layer of batter into the pan. The thickness should be approximately ¼ to ½ inches. It will rise slightly and bubble a little as it cooks. Cook until holes appear on the surface of the bread. Flip the injera and allow it to cook on both sides. Once the surface is dry, remove the bread from the pan to cool. Serve.

Note: injera can be frozen, thawed, and served for later.

EGYPT

At the top of Africa and to the east lies the country of Egypt. Egypt doesn't receive much rain (only 8 inches a year) and has no forests. Because of its arid climate, not many crops are grown there. Yet, wheat, barley, peas, beans, cucumbers, dates, figs, and grapes are all found frequently in Egyptian dishes. Traditional Egyptian dishes will usually also have bread, rice, and beans in them. Many people live along the Nile River, the second longest river in the world.

Koshari
~ Egypt's Unofficial National Dish ~
{serves 4–6}

Widely, but not officially, considered Egypt's national dish, koshari is a favorite food found everywhere from restaurants to street carts. Lentils (black or brown or even red), chickpeas, and pasta are cooked individually, then either layered or tossed together and topped with spiced tomato sauce and fried onions.

Packed with plant-based proteins of lentils and chickpeas, along with a hefty share of carbohydrates in the shape of rice and macaroni, this dish is both flavorful and filling, making it a favorite in our cooking classes.

For the Crispy Onion Topping
1 large onion, sliced into thin rings
all-purpose flour
salt
cooking oil

For Tomato Sauce
1 tablespoon olive oil
1 small yellow onion, finely chopped
3 garlic cloves, coarsely minced
1 teaspoon coriander
1 28 ounce can of crushed tomatoes
1 to 2 tablespoons white vinegar
½ teaspoon red pepper flakes (optional)
½ teaspoon sugar
½ teaspoon salt

For Base Layers
1 ½ cup lentils, rinsed
1 ½ cup medium grain rice
2 cups of elbow or macaroni pasta
Olive oil
1 15-oz can chickpeas, rinsed, drained and warmed

Lentils and Rice

Bring lentils and 4 cups of water to a boil in a medium pot or saucepan over high heat. Reduce the heat to low and cook until lentils are just tender (15–17 minutes). Drain from the water and season with a little salt. (Note: try not to overcook the lentils. They should still have a bite to them). Meanwhile, make the rice in a rice cooker or follow the package directions to make it on a stovetop. Mix rice and lentils over low heat. Add coriander and salt and mix. Keep covered and undisturbed for 5 minutes or so.

While the rice and lentils are cooking, make the pasta according to package instructions by adding the elbow pasta to boiling water with a dash of salt and a little oil. Cook until the pasta is al dente. Drain.

Chickpeas

Warm chickpeas in the microwave or in a saucepan with a little water briefly before serving.

Make the Tomato Sauce

In a medium saucepan, heat 1 tablespoon of cooking oil. Add the onion and cook on medium-high until the onion turns a translucent gold (do not brown). Now add the garlic, coriander, and red pepper flakes (if using), and saute about 1 minute. Stir in tomato sauce. Lower hear and cook until the sauce thickens (15 minutes or so). Stir in vinegar, salt, and sugar, and turn the heat to low. Cover and keep warm until ready to serve.

Fried Onions

Sprinkle the onion rings with salt, then toss them in the flour to coat. Shake off excess flour. In a large skillet, heat the cooking oil over medium-high heat, cook the onion rings, stirring often, until they turn a nice, caramelized brown. Onions must be crispy, but not burned (15-20 minutes).

Assemble

To serve, fluff the rice and lentils with a fork and transfer to a serving platter. Top with the elbow pasta, tomato sauce, then the chickpeas, and finally a few crispy onions for garnish. Serve, passing the remaining sauce and crispy onions separately.
SIDEBAR: Why add sugar? Sugar balances out the acidity of the tomatoes.

Om Ali
(traditional Egyptian bread pudding)
(serves 4 to 6)

Om Ali, a simple yet delicious Egyptian dessert, has as many origin stories as there are versions of the recipe. Here is one retelling of the story and one version. In the Resources section of our website, you'll find links to other versions of the story of its creation and recipes.

One day a sultan was on a hunting party through the Nile delta. He started to feel hungry. He stopped the hunting party and sent his soldiers in search of food. The soldiers came upon a poor village explaining that the sultan would soon be on his way to their village and that he was very hungry. The villagers ran to find their best cook, Om'Ali, with the hopes that the chef could help feed the hungry sultan. She filled a large pan with the little food they had – scrapings of stale wheat flakes with bits of nuts – and put it in the oven together with milk and sugar. The sultan loved the dish so much that he went back to the village on his next hunting party and several more times after. The dessert soon became the sultan's favorite and was named Om Ali, after its creator.

8 sheets filo dough pastry
½ cup pistachios, chopped
2 tablespoons sugar
2 tablespoons shredded coconut flakes
1 can sweetened condensed milk
½ cup heavy cream
1 ½ cups milk
1 teaspoon rosewater (optional but recommended)
pomegranate seeds (if out of season, substitute with dried cranberries or barberries)

Preheat the oven to 400F. Scrunch each filo sheet into a ball and place flakes of dough on a cookie sheet pan lined with parchment paper. Bake for 10 minutes or until golden. Leave the oven on at the same temperature. Heat condensed milk, cream, and milk in a saucepan over medium heat until warm but not boiling. Stir in rosewater and remove from heat. Using six small oven-safe ramekins, scatter baked filo flakes with nuts, sugar, and coconut. Pour milk mixture into ramekins over the filo, nuts, and sugar. Bake for 15 minutes or until golden brown on top. Serve with pomegranate seeds on top.

If you don't have ramekins, you can make this recipe in a well-oiled or buttered shallow baking dish.

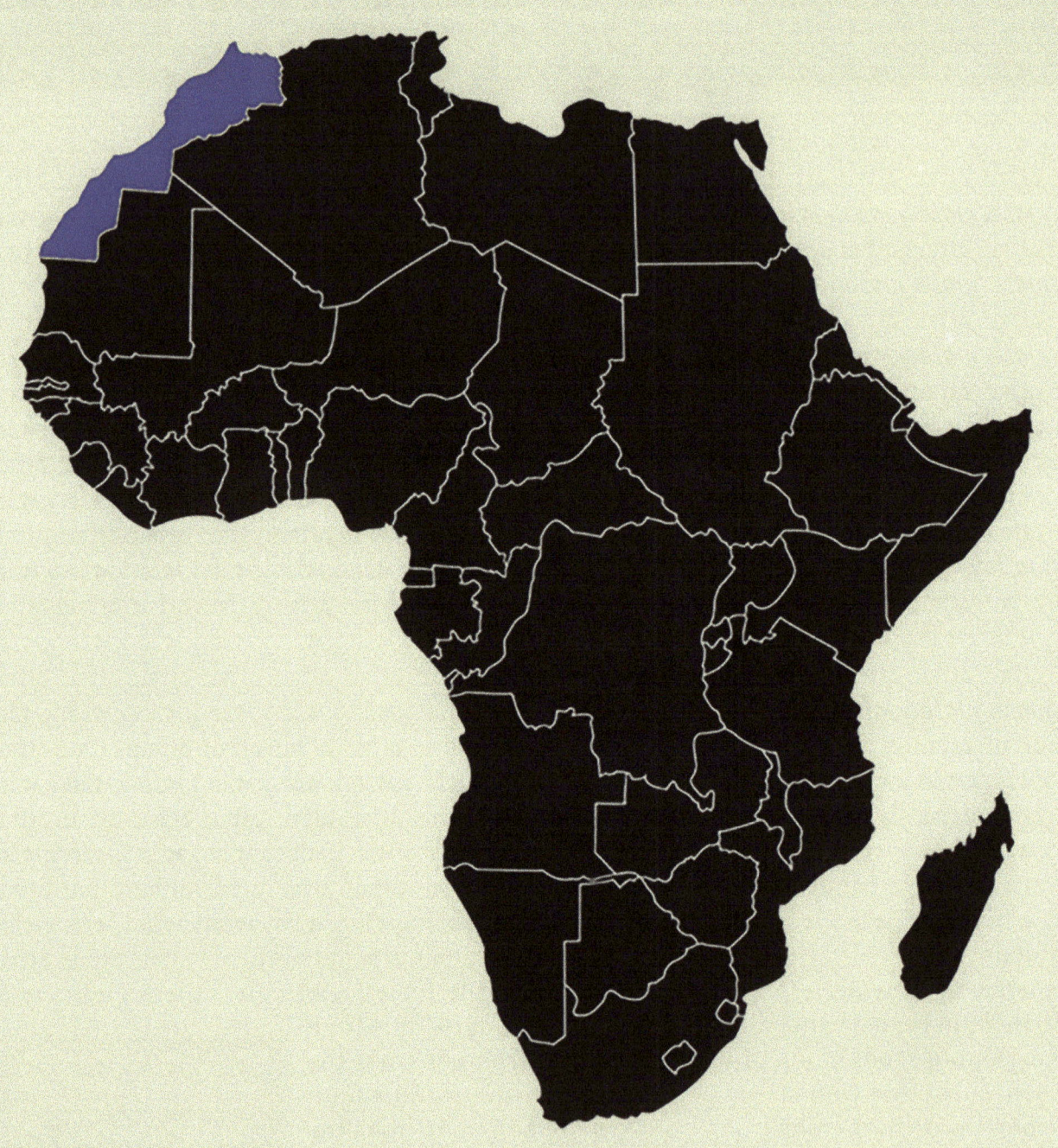

MOROCCO

Morocco is a mountainous country situated in the northwestern part of Africa. It lies directly across the Strait of Gibraltar from Spain. Its location near Europe and along the Atlantic Ocean make it a place of movement and migration. It is often seen as a crossroads between Europe, the Middle East and Africa. And its cuisine reflects the best of these places yet somehow manages to be unique at the same time.

Tomatoes, peppers, onions, and eggplants are just some of the varieties of vegetables used in Moroccan dishes. And then there are the spices. We included a Moroccan spice blend which we feature in our Radical Cooks herbs and spices classes. I personally use it to season anything from meats to tofu to jackfruit.

Couscous
(serves 4 to 6)

GRAIN OR PASTA?

Couscous is almost synonymous with Morocco. It a staple in the country. No one knows the exact origin of couscous but some say it was created by the Berbers. Today is and although the origin of couscous is unknown, it perhaps was created by the Berbers. Today it is typically served with meat or vegetable stew, mixed with nuts and dried fruit. However, it can also be eaten by itself.

While it is often sold on grocery store shelves near the grains, it is actually a type of pasta. Made with semolina flour, couscous comes in different sizes, ranging from fine small shapes to larger, pearled balls of pasta. Serve it toasted, plain, with herbs or spices, or both.

2 tablespoons extra virgin olive oil
1 1/2 teaspoon minced garlic (1 large clove)
1 1/4 cups vegetable broth
Zest from one lemon
fresh lemon juice from one lemon
Salt
2 tablespoons chopped fresh parsley, or more to taste
1 cup (6 oz) couscous (not pearl couscous)

Other herbs you can try with couscous include mint, oregano, or basil Also, consider adding nuts, such as pine nuts or chopped almonds

Heat olive oil in a medium saucepan over medium-low heat. Add garlic and saute until fragrant (don't let it brown or garlic will be bitter!), about 20 seconds. Remove from heat, pour in the broth, lemon zest, and lemon juice, and season with salt to taste. Place over medium-high heat and bring to a boil. Pour in couscous, stir, then remove from heat and immediately cover with lid. Let it rest 5 minutes off heat. Add parsley and fluff with a fork. Finish with a little more olive oil or broth to moisten if desired and serve warm.

Moroccan Spice Blend

There are many different versions of what we call a Moroccan spice blend. Use this one as your base or experiment making your own. It is a great spice blend to add to roasted chicken, potatoes, or vegetables. The goal is to find a perfect balance of warming spices, such as ginger, cinnamon, and hotter spices such as pepper and cayenne.

1 teaspoon ground cumin
1 teaspoon ground ginger
1 teaspoon salt
¾ teaspoon black pepper
½ teaspoon ground cinnamon
½ teaspoon ground coriander

½ teaspoon ground cayenne pepper
½ teaspoon ground allspice
¼ teaspoon ground cloves

Mix and serve on potatoes, tofu, vegetables, meats, and more.

WHAT IS A TAGINE?

A tagine, sometimes spelled "tajine," depending upon one's perspective, is either a hot dish or a cooking vessel. It is iconic to Moroccan cooking. The cooking vessel is traditionally made of ceramic or unglazed clay with a round base and low sides with a cone-shaped cover that sits on the base. The lid traps steam during cooking and returns the liquid to the dish, resulting in a moist dish with concentrated flavors. It is perfect for slow-cooked savory stews or chicken. While it is a wonderful addition to a kitchen if you want to be truly authentic to Moroccan or other North African cuisines it is not a necessity to make the following recipe. In our classes, we often get by using a Dutch oven or stock pot. I will admit they are beautiful in shape and color and would be a fun international twist to your kitchen equipment.

Moroccan Vegetable Stew
(serve 6 to 8)

I make this stew throughout the winter months. During an ambitious meal prep session, I will double the recipe, divide it into small batches, freeze and thaw and eat as the winter weeks progress. It's warm and inviting and easy to reheat and serve.

Ingredients

1 large onion, yellow, white or purple
3 cloves garlic
½ head cauliflower, chopped
2 zucchini, diced into large cubes
2 carrots, sliced or diced
1 red sweet pepper, diced in large pieces
2 large sweet potatoes (about 1 ¾ pound), diced (leave skins on)
2 tablespoons olive oil
2 tablespoons Moroccan spice mix
1 15-ounce can of diced tomatoes
2 cups vegetable broth
15-ounce can chickpeas, drained and rinsed (or 1 1/2 cups cooked)
2 cups spinach, chard, or kale, chopped
2 tablespoons chopped fresh cilantro or parsley, for garnish
1 lemon, for garnish

Roast potatoes, carrots, cauliflower, and zucchini in an oven preheated to 400F. Meanwhile, dice onion and mince 3 cloves of garlic. In a large pot, heat 2 tablespoons of olive oil. Saute the onion for about 5 minutes. Add minced garlic and saute about 1 minute. Stir in spice mix, then add diced tomatoes, chickpeas, and 2 cups broth. Bring to a boil, then rinsed chickpeas. When vegetables are roasted (15-20 minutes), stir in. Serve over couscous, quinoa or other whole grain with lemon garnish, sour cream or plain yogurt.

EUROPE

According to National Geographic, Europe, the sixth-largest continent, contains just seven percent of the world's land. Yet, the population of Europe is more than twice that of South America. Europe has more than 40 countries and many of the world's major cities, including London, the United Kingdom; Paris, France; Berlin, Germany; Rome, Italy; Madrid, Spain; and Moscow, Russia.

The continent is bordered by the Arctic Ocean in the north, the Atlantic Ocean in the west, the Caspian Sea in the southeast, and the Mediterranean and Black Seas in the south. The nearness of these bodies of water and the navigation of many of Europe's rivers played a major role in this continent's history. The early Europeans' ability to navigate and explore outside of Europe was an important part of its social, cultural, and linguistic history and the impact they had on other continents, including even the explorations of Antarctica.

In terms of cuisine, we will explore Italy, Greece, France, and Ireland.

ITALY

For many people living outside of Italy, its cuisine is thought to consist of pizza and pasta. It is so much more. Until 1861 Italy wasn't even a country. It was a collection of towns and villages and city-states. The residents of these city-states ate according to their local climate and geography. In the north, regions we now know as Friuli Venezia Giulia or Piedmont served dishes of wild game, rice, and polenta. In the south, closer to the oceanic trade routes, fish was a main part of the daily diet. Today there is much overlap in modern Italian cuisine but if you travel to Italy and visit different regions you will learn that even one plate of pasta can be different from one region to the next. For regional traditions permeate the culture allowing us to appreciate the differences in food from place to place.

Potato Gnocchi
(serves 6–8)

My mother's family was from northern Italy and she made the most delicious northern Italian food. Each year my mother would offer to make something special for dinner on my birthday. Every year I requested the same thing ~ gnocchi. It was a time-consuming and hands-on adventure in the kitchen. It was also special to her as her family came from northern Italy, which is where they say gnocchi was invented.

Ingredients are simple. Mastering technique takes time. Specialty equipment you might want to have on hand would be a potato ricer and a gnocchi paddle. I did not use either growing up but we use both in our classes as the ricer removes any clumps and the paddle is, quite honestly, just really fun to use.

When we make this dish in our cooking classes students are amazed at how light and fluffy homemade gnocchi can be. Those who may have had gnocchi before have usually had the store-bought version which often turns out to be very chewy and rubbery. Good homemade gnocchi is a pillowy bit of heaven, as one of my students described it. Try this recipe and challenge yourself in creating pillowy bits of heaven.

2 (8 ounces approximately) Russet potatoes
1/2 teaspoon salt
1 egg
2 cups all-purpose flour

Preheat the oven to 400 degrees F (175 degrees C). Bake potatoes for 50 minutes. Remove from the oven, and set aside to cool. Bring a large pot of lightly salted water to a boil. While the water comes to a boil, make the gnocchi. Once the potatoes are cool enough to work with, remove the peels, and mash them, or press them through a potato ricer into a large bowl. Mix in the flour and egg a little at a time until you have a soft dough. Use more or less flour as needed.

On a floured surface, roll the dough out in several long snakes or ropes, and cut into 1-inch sections. Using your thumb, roll each piece down over the tines of a fork or gnocchi paddle to indent.

Drop the pieces into the boiling water, and allow them to cook until they float to the surface. Place on a plate and keep warm and serve with sauce of your choice.

Pesto Sauce

In my humble opinion, the only thing better than fresh basil is fresh basil turned into pesto. In the summer months, we make this sauce in class and use it for gnocchi, pizza, and more. Purists will say you should not use a blender or food processor. I am not a purist. Use a food processor if it suits you.

1 cup pine nuts or almonds or walnuts
3 cups basil leaves
1/2 cup grated pecorino or Parmesan cheese
3 garlic cloves, roughly chopped
1/2 teaspoon salt
1/2 cup olive oil

Put the nuts, basil, cheese, garlic, and salt in a food processor and pulse for a few seconds to combine. Scrape down the sides of the bowl, then pulse again. Drizzle in the olive oil while the machine is running just long enough to incorporate the oil, about 20–30 seconds. Use immediately or cover with plastic wrap and refrigerate to store. It will last several days chilled. Makes about 1 to 2 cups.

Italian Wedding Cookies

These are the cookies I grew up making. It was one of the first recipes I did on my own. These cookies are simple, and delicious, and I promise you they will disappear in minutes!

1 1/2 cups unsalted butter
3/4 cup confectioners' sugar (also known as powdered sugar)
3/4 teaspoon salt
1 1/2 cups chopped walnuts
4 1/2 teaspoons vanilla extract
3 cups sifted all-purpose flour
1/3 cup confectioners' sugar for rolling

Preheat the oven to 325 degrees F (165 degrees C). Cream butter in a bowl, and gradually add confectioners' sugar and salt. Beat until light and fluffy. Add nuts and vanilla. Blend in flour gradually mixing well. Wrap the dough in plastic and chill for at least 2 hours. Remove from the refrigerator and shape the dough into balls (or crescents) using about 1 teaspoon for each cookie. Place on a cookie sheet pan lined with parchment paper, and bake for 15-20 minutes. Do not brown. Allow to cool on a metal rack and sift confectioner's sugar over cookies. Serve. Makes about 40 cookies.

GREECE

Located in the southeastern part of Europe, on the southern end of the Balkan Peninsula (Haemus peninsula), **Greece** lies at the meeting point of three continents – Europe, Asia, and Africa.

It is said that the ancient Greek culture was the birthplace of Western civilization about 4000 years ago. Ancient Greece produced amazing achievements in the area of government, science, philosophy, and cooking. Yes, cooking! In fact, a Greek, Archestratus, is thought to have written the first cookbook in 350 BCE.

Greek cooking traditions date back thousands of years and Greeks today eat some of the same dishes and often use the same ingredients as their ancestors. Some of these include:

Olive oil. This monosaturated oil is produced from olive trees prominent throughout the region and adds to the distinctive taste of Greek food.

Lemons. The Greek islands are full of lemon trees and so lemons are used with everything from soups to sauces to steaks.

Oregano. The word oregano comes from the Greek word "oros" which means mountain or hill, and "ganos," meaning "brightness or joy." In Greek mythology, Aphrodite, the goddess of Love, created oregano as a symbol of happiness and grew it in her garden in Mt. Olympus. At traditional Greek weddings, the bride and groom are crowned with wreaths of oregano.

Greek Salad
(horiatiki)
(serves 2 to 4)

I first learned to make a Greek salad in, of all places, southern Illinois. I was in college taking a French class and met a fellow student who was from Greece. She needed help editing her dissertation as her knowledge of English was not that strong. I needed help with my French, which she was fluent in. She invited me over for dinner and together we cooked and laughed and learned French and English. Along the way, I learned how to make a Greek salad, spanokopita, and rosemary lemon chicken. While I do hope to travel to Greece one day my experiences in southern Illinois are a lesson that you don't necessarily have to travel to a country to learn the cuisine. You just need to be open to meeting new people and invite yourself over for dinner.

A traditional Greek salad is a combination of a few simple ingredients: tomatoes, cucumbers, bell peppers, red onions, olives, and blocks of creamy feta cheese. Cut your vegetables into cut large chunks. Don't forget the oregano for the vinaigrette.

2 medium-sized tomatoes, cut into wedges
1 English cucumber *(or two small Persian cucumbers)*, sliced into half-moons
1 large green bell pepper, cored and sliced into chunks
½ small red onion, peeled and thinly sliced
1/2 cup kalamata olives
3-4 tablespoons olive oil
2 tablespoons red wine vinegar
1 teaspoon dried or fresh oregano, plus extra for serving
sea salt
5 ounces feta cheese, cubed

After slicing vegetables into large slices or chunks, plate onto a rimmed platter or bowl. Toss olives on top of the vegetables. Add feta cheese cubes. Sprinkle kosher salt and dried oregano on top. Drizzle extra virgin olive oil and a splash of red wine vinegar on top. Salt to taste and serve.

Zucchini Fritters
(Makes 12 small fritters)

In our children's classes, we enjoy making these fritters because they are so hands-on. Everyone has a job to do, from grating the zucchini to squeezing out the liquid to mixing the batter and more. And you simply must include the dip. Grab a group of friends and try them out yourself.

Ingredients

1 pound zucchini (about 2 medium)
1 teaspoon salt
2 large eggs
2 scallions or green onions, minced
2 tablespoons fresh oregano
½ cup crumbled feta cheese
1 medium garlic clove, minced
¼ teaspoon black pepper
¼ cup cornstarch or all-purpose flour
½ teaspoon baking powder
Oil for frying
Lemon wedges for serving

Top and tail and then grate zucchini. Add grated zucchini to a fine mesh sieve strainer and set over a bowl. Toss the zucchini with the salt and let it sit for 10 minutes. Wring all of the excess liquid out of the zucchini with your hands, then set it aside. You can also use a cheesecloth to extract as much water as possible. Beat the egg in a large bowl. Mix in the dried zucchini, scallions, dill, feta, garlic, and black pepper. Sprinkle the corn starch or flour and baking powder over the mixture and stir until incorporated.

Heat some oil in a large non-stick skillet over medium heat. Drop 2-tablespoon-sized portions into the pan and spread into 2-inch wide fritters. Pan fry until golden brown on both sides, about 2-3 minutes. Continue the process until the batter is gone. Serve with lemon wedges and tzatziki.

"TZATZIKI"
Greek yogurt dip

½ of a large cucumber, unpeeled or 2 Persian cucumbers
1 ½ cups plain full-fat Greek yogurt
2 tablespoons extra virgin olive oil
1 tablespoon white vinegar
½ teaspoon salt
1 tablespoon minced fresh dill
2 large garlic cloves, finely minced (optional)
Pepper, to taste

> This dip can be served immediately or can be refrigerated overnight. If you refrigerate overnight the taste of the garlic will be milder.

Grate the cucumber and drain through a fine-mesh sieve for 10 minutes, squeezing out any excess liquid with your hands (if you have the time, drain in the fridge overnight). Combine yogurt, oil, vinegar, garlic, and salt in a large bowl. Transfer grated and drained cucumber and fresh dill into the yogurt mixture and stir to combine. Serve chilled.

FRANCE

France is a country located in the northwestern part of Europe. It has a rich history and is considered one of the world's oldest nations. When it comes to cooking, many might say France wrote the book, albeit possibly not the first one (see notes on Greece). France, or French chefs, have indeed written a lot of books on cooking. And the ability to "master" French cuisine has for many years been considered the gold standard by which many chefs have been judged. French cuisine has been a major influence on cooking around the world and continues to be an influence today. That said, I have a to brag a little. When we last made these crepes in class, one student remarked they were better than the ones he had in Paris. Huge praise, indeed.

My Favorite Crepes
(serves 4)

While it was hard to choose just one recipe for France, I decided to follow the structure of our classes, beginning simply, with the quintessential crepe.

The word crepe comes from the Latin word *crispus* meaning "curled." Crepes originated in Brittany in the northwest region of France. Traditionally, on February 2nd every French home would make dozen of lovely crepes to eat together. It was believed to be for the return of the light of spring and it is called "La Chandeleur".

A crêpe is an unleavened, flat, thin pancake of cooked dough or batter, which is used as a wrapper for another food. Crêpe batter is generally made from flour, eggs, milk, butter, salt, sugar (sometimes), water, and oil. Simple ingredients with a technique to master is the essence of many French recipes and crepes are no exception.

1 cup flour
2 eggs
1 cup milk
¼ cup water
4 tablespoons butter
pinch of salt

Sift the flour and salt into a mixing bowl. Make a well in the center of the flour. Break the eggs into the well. Whisk the eggs and flour together. Next, mix together the water and milk in a separate bowl or large measuring cup. Add the liquid to the flour, a little at a time, whisking to make a smooth batter. Melt two tablespoons of the butter and stir it into the batter. Strain if lumpy. Melt a pat of butter into a frying pan. Be sure to get the pan really hot, then turn down the heat to medium. Add the batter, about two tablespoons. Tilt the pan so that the batter covers the base and cook the crepe for about one minute. Using a spatula to loosen it, flip it over and cook the second side for about 30 seconds. Fill the crepes with fresh fruit, syrup, whipped cream, etc.

> Do you need to add sugar to your crepe batter? I think not, especially if you're making a sweet crepe. There will be enough sugar from the fruit, syrup, cream, etc.

IRELAND

Ireland, officially known as the Republic of Ireland, occupies most of the island, also known as Ireland, in the North Atlantic. It is separated from Great Britain to its east by the North Channel, the Irish Sea, and St George's Channel. Just over 4 million people inhabit this island. It has been characterized as a Catholic majority country, although only a small percentage of the current population regularly attends church.

If you were to ask chefs to name their favorite world cuisine Irish cuisine may not readily roll off their tongues. In fact, many might say it wouldn't be in their top five or even fifteen. Yet, good food isn't always about the most famous or trendiest food. A delicious meal can be found in the simplest of homes and the most rustic of places. Irish food meets this definition in many ways and you can celebrate its offerings with the simplest of ingredients ~ the potato.

Colcannon
{4 servings}

Colcannon is traditionally made from mashed potatoes and kale (or cabbage), with milk, cream, butter, salt, and pepper. It can contain other ingredients such as scallions, leeks, or chives, and is often served with boiled ham or Irish bacon. An Irish Halloween tradition is to serve colcannon with a ring and thimble hidden in the dish. I would not try this tradition unless everyone is in on the game so as to avoid a choking incident at the table.

This recipe uses kale because I love kale. It is a great way to have your family eat more leafy greens.

5 medium Yukon Gold potatoes (about 1¾ pounds), skins on
Kosher salt
6 tablespoons unsalted butter, divided
2 leeks or green onions, thinly sliced crosswise
2 garlic cloves, thinly sliced
2 cups (packed) chopped kale
1¼ cups milk
½ cup heavy cream
Freshly ground black pepper
1 scallion or green onion, thinly sliced

Quarter potatoes, leaving skins on. Cover potatoes with water in a pot and season with salt. Bring to a boil over medium-high heat, then reduce heat and simmer until a paring knife slides easily through the flesh of the potato. This will take about 30–40 minutes. Drain, let cool slightly, and set aside.

Meanwhile, melt 4 tablespoons of butter in a large saucepan over medium heat. Add leeks and cook, stirring frequently, until very soft, about 8–10 minutes. Add garlic and cook, stirring frequently, until garlic is fragrant and leeks are just beginning to brown. Add 1 cup of kale and cook, stirring constantly, until wilted. Add milk and cream and bring to a simmer. Add potatoes and the remaining 1 cup of kale, then coarsely mash with a potato masher. Season with salt and pepper.

> For a healthier version, substitute the cream with almond milk and use coconut oil instead of butter or vegan butter. Leaving the skins on the potatoes also helps retain vitamins and minerals.

Plate colcannon into a large serving bowl. Top with remaining butter and sprinkle with scallions.

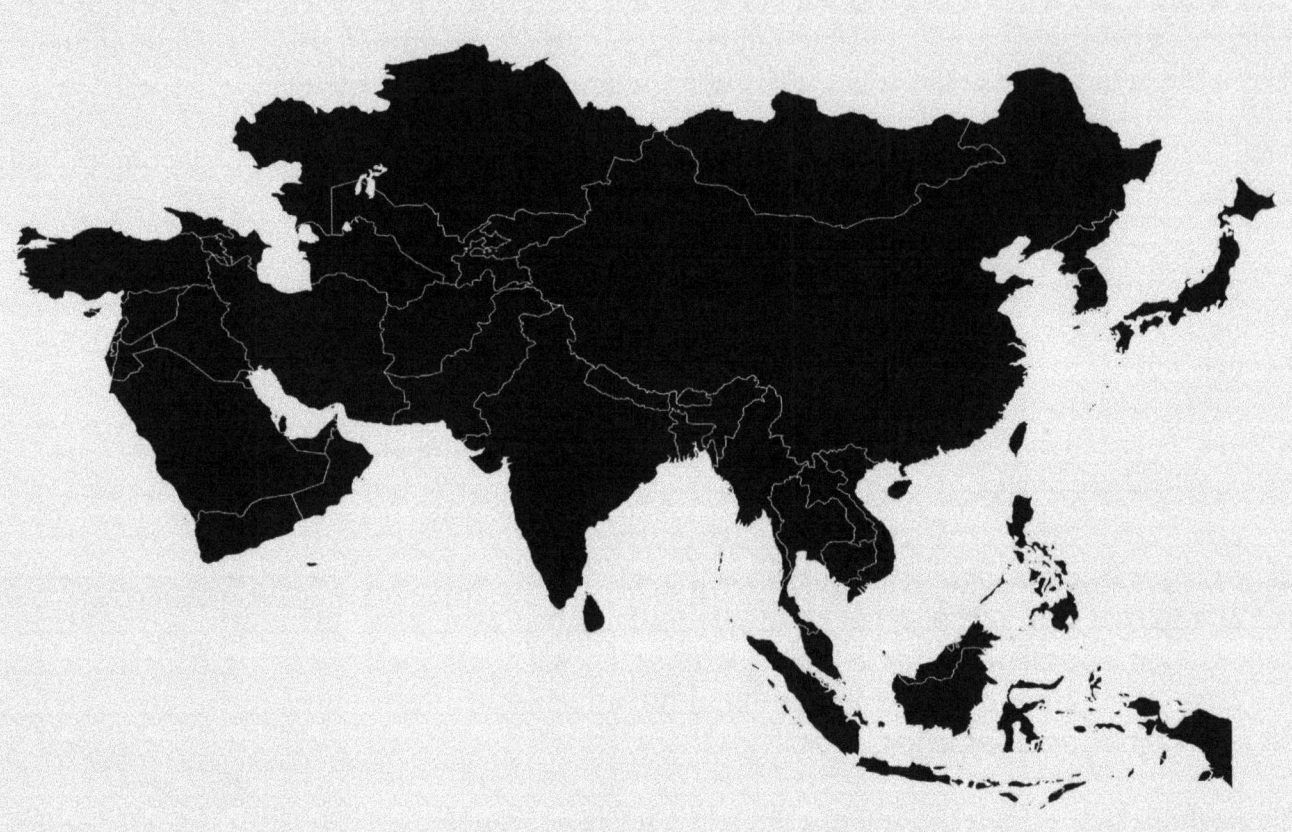

ASIA

Asia ~ it's the world's largest and most populated continent (an estimated 4.4 billion people so far!!!!). Asia has just about every climate you can think of. It boasts the highest peak (Mount Everest) and the largest city by population (Tokyo).

There is a lot to love about this continent, most especially the different types of cuisine which can be found in its many different countries. Because it is such a large continent, we decided to feature a few more countries from this continent ~ Japan, China, Vietnam, India, and Vietnam.

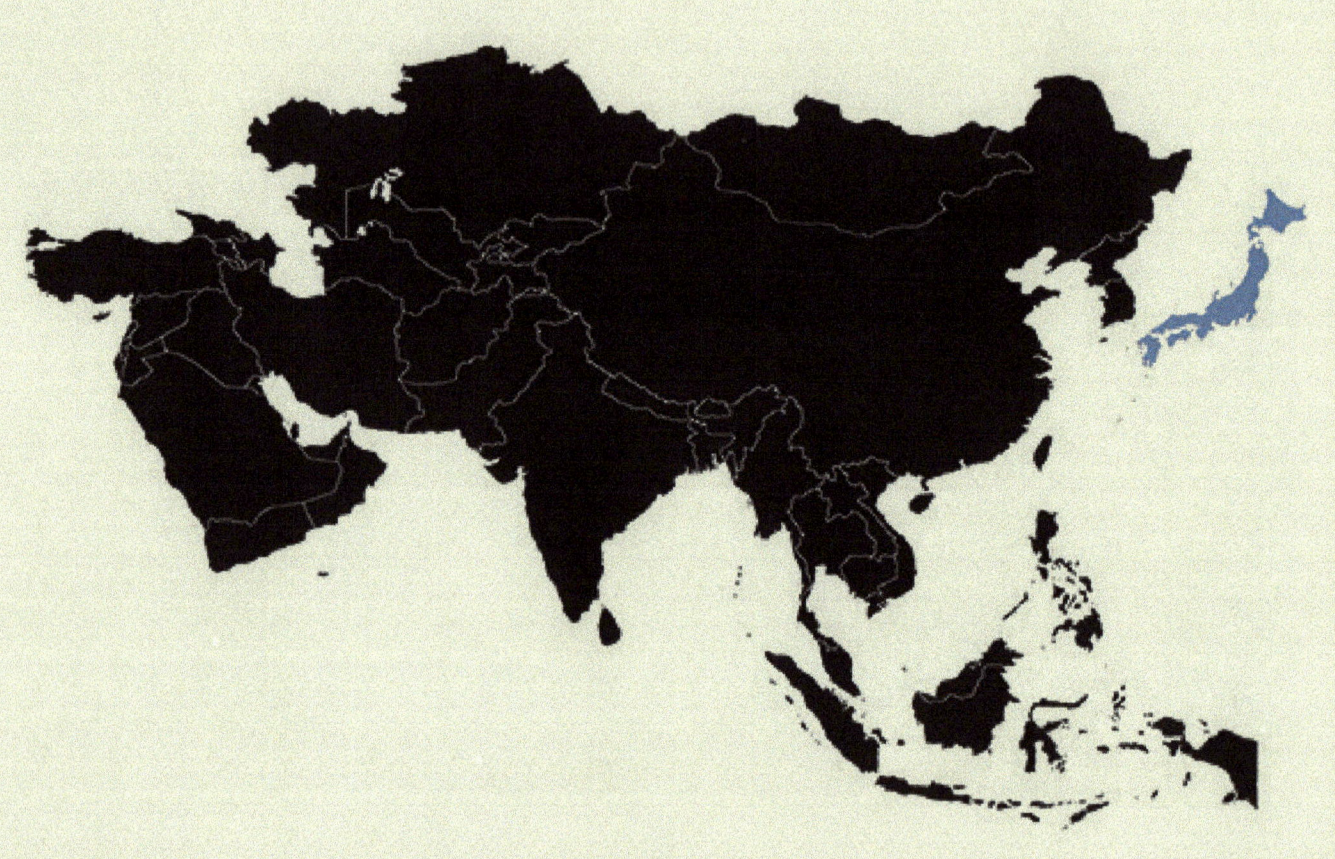

JAPAN

Japan is an island country located to the west of the mainland of Asia. It's actually four large islands and thousands of smaller ones and has everything from snow-capped mountains to sandy shores. Consequently, there are some big differences in diet and cooking styles between the regions of Japan. Despite the differences though, there lies a common ground ~ the ocean. No matter where you might find yourself in Japan, you'll discover there are plenty of fish and other marine products found in Japanese food. Seafood, seaweed, and sea salt are often key ingredients in Japanese cuisine. Also, with the climate perfect for growing rice, the Japanese diet consists of rice as a staple food, with fish and veggies rounding out the meal.

As I explain to our students when it comes to describing the Japanese diet, think "natural" & "harmony." Whatever dish is made, the Japanese strive to never kill the natural flavor of the ingredients. The ingredients are often found in harmony together to make one dish. Analyze the cuisine further, and you will notice dishes are often in harmony with other dishes to make a meal.

Simple Sushi Nori Maki
(serves 5 to 6)

Sushi is probably the most famous Japanese dish outside of Japan. In Japan, sushi is usually enjoyed on special occasions, such as birthday celebrations. While sushi is typically defined as a dish containing rice seasoned with rice vinegar, it's important to understand there are many different types of sushi, with raw fish or vegetables or both.

One of the most common and popular is norimaki. It is sushi rice and seafood or vegetables rolled in dried seaweed sheets. For this recipe, it helps to have a sushi bamboo rolling mat but it's not mandatory. Before delving into expensive sashimi-grade fish while you are learning to roll sushi, I recommend starting with a cucumber roll. As you improve upon your rolling technique then you can add more expensive ingredients such as sashimi grade fish and try different types of sushi.

5 sheets nori seaweed
2 cups "sushi" rice (recipe below)
1 small cucumber, cut into thin, long strips

Wrap your rolling mat in plastic wrap, then place a nori sheet lengthwise on the mat, shiny side down. Position the sheet about ½ inch from the edge of the mat, leaving some of the bamboo mat exposed on either side of the nori sheet. Wet your hands in cool water seasoned with rice wine vinegar and take a handful of the rice. . Place the rice in the center of the nori sheet. Using your fingers or rice paddle spread the rice evenly over the nori. Be sure to leave ¾ inch strip of nori uncovered on the far side. Place strips of cucumber along near the edge of the seaweed closest to you, about 1 to 2 inches away from the edge of the piece of seaweed. Do not overfill. You only need one layer of rice. Sliding your thumbs under the mat to lift up the edge of the bamboo rolling mat closest to you, begin rolling the mat away from you, while applying pressure with your remaining fingers to the fillings to keep the roll firm. Roll the mat over until it covers the rice, leaving the ¾-inch strip of nori rice free, exposed. While holding the bamboo mat in position, apply pressure to the roll to make it firm. Slice the roll in half, and then cut both rolls twice to make six equal-sized pieces. Repeat.

> Why have a bowl of water with rice vinegar on hand? The water mixed with vinegar helps remove the sticky grains of rice stuck to your hands.

Sushi Rice

Sushi rice is not a type of rice as much as it is seasoned rice of small or medium grade size. You can buy the seasoning pre-made at some Japanese markets or you can make your own, following the recipe here.

I highly recommend investing in a rice cooker. I've had one for so long that I can't remember the last time I made rice on the stove. Once you purchase one, you can use it for cooking other types of grains, too.

1 cup short or medium grain rice
3-4 tablespoons rice vinegar
1 tablespoon sugar
1 teaspoon salt

First, wash your rice at least three times in a fine mesh strainer. Then place 1 cup rice with 1 1/2 cups of cold water into the rice cooker and cook until done. In a saucepan heat vinegar, sugar, and salt together until sugar and salt are dissolved. Once the rice is done pour into a bowl or sushi tub. While the rice is still hot, mix in vinegar, sugar, and salt mixture into the rice using a spatula or rice paddle being careful not to crush the grains of rice while mixing. Let cool and use to make sushi.

Okonomiyaki

Okonomiyaki means, I am told, "to one's liking," It is a popular pan-fried food that consists of flour and egg batter, and cabbage. Toppings and ingredients are added which can vary greatly (anything from meat and seafood to wasabi and cheese) to create a savory pancake. You'll often see it topped with pork or bacon.

This dish is available throughout Japan, but it is most popular in the west, particularly in the

About Okonomiyaki flour

You can buy this flour at Japanese grocery stores. What makes it special is added starch to help it bind and make a better pancake. You can also make your own by mixing five tablespoons of flour with 1 tablespoon of baking powder and then adding about 5 tablespoons of water to form the batter.

cities of Hiroshima and Osaka. In fact, each city has its own version of the dish. There are restaurants that specialize in okonomiyaki in the same way there are restaurants that specialize in making pizza in other parts of the world. I only wish there were as many okonomiyaki restaurants as there are pizza restaurants.

In our classes, we like to keep most recipes vegetarian to be more inclusive so we will omit the bonito flakes and substitute shitake mushrooms for bacon. Either way, the okonomiyaki is so good. At home I serve it with a cold Japanese beer.

1 cup Okonomiyaki flour
2 eggs
3 spring onions, diced
¼ tenkasu (tempura bits)
2/3 cup vegetable stock
3 cups cabbage cut into thin strips
2 tablespoons vegetable oil
Slices of fresh or rehydrated shitake mushrooms, if vegetarian, or slices of pork belly or bacon

What is tenkasu?
Tenkasu are crunchy tempura scraps of deep-fried batter. They add a crunchy texture to okonomiyaki.

Toppings

Kewpie mayonnaise
Bonito Flakes
Okonomi sauce

In a large bowl, whisk together the okonomiyaki flour and stock until smooth. Add eggs, cabbage, onions, and tenkasu and mix. Spread oil in a very hot frypan and divide the mixture into 4 flattened circles in the frypan. Add mushroom slices or bacon slices to cover the top of each pancake. After about 3 minutes, flip the pancake over onto the bacon side. Cook for 4 minutes. Flip the pancake over again and cook for a further minute until browned and firm. Place on a serving plate, drizzle with kewpie mayonnaise, okonomi sauce and then sprinkle with bonito flakes or seaweed.

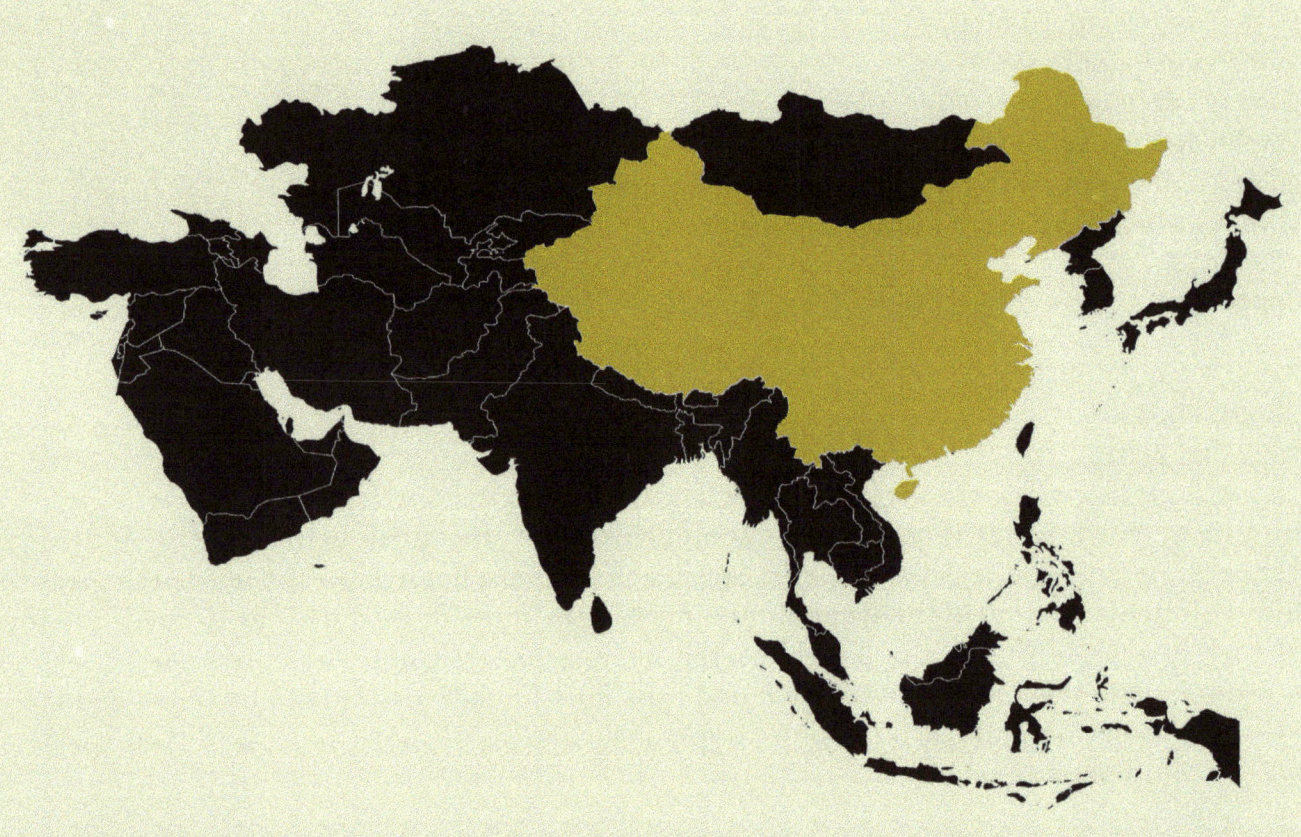

CHINA

A country the size of China, with the largest population on the continent of Asia, cannot be easily summarized in a paragraph, and neither can its cuisine. As with other large countries, its cuisine is regional and diverse. To give tribute to China, I go back to my roots.

Growing up in small-town America, the idea of going to, let alone finding, a Chinese restaurant was an exotic adventure. Using chopsticks, and ordering dishes with strange vegetables like bamboo shoots and baby corn was new and exciting. Back home I would try to replicate the fortune cookie, with epic disasters. One dish successfully migrated from restaurant to home kitchen with our family ~ the stir fry.

Stir Fry
(serves 4 to 6)

More technique than a recipe, fresh ingredients like vegetables and mushrooms, are fried in a small amount of oil, being stirred or tossed until cooked. The essence of a good stir fry, in my opinion, is flavor and freshness.

In addition to being quick and easy, stir-frying is also healthy. A good stirfy has tender-crisp vegetables that retain more nutrients than if they were boiled. And since stir-frying requires only a small amount of oil, the fat content is low. We use firm tofu to make the dish vegetarian, but you can use pork or chicken. Making a stir fry is a great way to practice your knife skills, too.

Cook's Tip: To help cook the vegetables at the same rate, make sure to cut into similar and smaller-sized pieces

Ingredients will vary, but typical stir fry is broken down into the following parts:

- **Oil**
- **Vegetables**: red bell pepper, yellow bell peppers, sugar snap peas, carrots, mushrooms, broccoli, baby corn, water chestnuts.
- **Protein:** tofu, chicken, beef, or pork
- **Sauce**: soy sauce, garlic cloves (minced), sugar (optional), sesame oil, water or broth, cornstarch
- **Garnish**: green onions, sesame seeds

1 packet of firm tofu
1 tablespoon oil
snow peas or snap peas
carrots, sliced on the bias
mushrooms sliced
broccoli, sliced
baby corn
water chestnuts, sliced

¼ cup soy sauce
3 garlic cloves minced
1 to 2 teaspoons minced ginger
1 teaspoon sesame oil
1/2 cup water or broth
1 tablespoon cornstarch
chopped green onions and sesame seeds for garnish optional

In a small whisk together soy sauce, garlic, sesame oil, water or broth, and cornstarch. After vegetables are chopped or minced, in a wok or large skillet add 1 tablespoon oil over medium-high heat. Once the oil is hot but not smoking, add onions and carrots and saute for 2 to 3 minutes until veggies are almost tender. Add broccoli, mushrooms, baby corn, and water chestnuts. Sauté another 2-3 minutes until veggies are almost tender. Add tofu.

Pour sauce over veggies and cook until the sauce has thickened. Garnish with chopped green onions and sesame seeds if desired. Serve over rice or noodles.

VIETNAM

How fortunate am I to have been able to travel to Vietnam in 1999? It was my first time traveling to Southeast Asia. We traveled to the mountains of the north around a place called Sapa and took a boat ride to the Cat Ba Islands. During these travels I fell in love with the people and the countryside and, of course, the food. In my experience I found that the best food in Vietnam wasn't in the fancy restaurants. It was in the alley or the back streets. And the best street food is the fresh spring (or summer) roll.

Vietnamese Spring Or "Summer" Rolls

(serve 4 to 6 with one to two rolls per person)

In Vietnamese, fresh spring or summer rolls made with rice paper are called gỏi cuốn, translating to "salad rolls" (gỏi means "salad" and cuốn means "to coil" or "to roll"). While a spring roll is said to have originated in China, the Vietnamese version is made of rice paper, softened (not cooked or fried!) in the water, and rolled around a filling of rice vermicelli, raw vegetables, and fresh herbs like Vietnamese basil, coriander, and mint, with a protein (tofu, shrimp, chicken, or pork), and served with a dipping sauce.

1 package of rice vermicelli
8 rice wrappers (8.5 inch diameter)
1 package of baked or firm tofu, cut in long strips, 2 inches long and 1/8" wide
sprigs of fresh Thai basil (or regular basil)
sprigs of fresh mint leaves
sprigs of fresh coriander (or cilantro)

Two dipping sauces

Mix the following:
1/4 cup water
2 tablespoons fresh lime juice
1 clove of garlic, minced
2 tablespoons white sugar (optional)
1/2 teaspoon garlic chili sauce
3 tablespoons hoisin sauce

OR

For a peanut sauce, add ½ cup of creamy peanut butter and top with chopped peanuts

> **Is it a spring or summer roll?**
>
> The terms get confused and are sometimes used interchangeably. Summer rolls are a type of roll that is wrapped in rice paper and NOT fried. But we have also found these unfriend and fresh rolls to be called spring rolls.

Bring a medium saucepan of water to boil. Turn off the gas and soak rice vermicelli for 3 to 5 minutes, or until al dente, and drain. Fill a large bowl with warm water. Dip one wrapper into the hot water for 20 to 30 seconds to soften. Lay the wrapper flat. In a row across the center, place 2 strips of tofu or other protein, a handful of vermicelli, basil, mint, and cilantro, leaving about 2 inches uncovered on each side. Fold uncovered sides inward, then tightly roll the wrapper, beginning at the end with the lettuce. Repeat with remaining ingredients. In a small bowl, mix the hoisin sauce, lime juice, garlic, sugar and chili sauce. Serve rolled spring rolls with sauce.

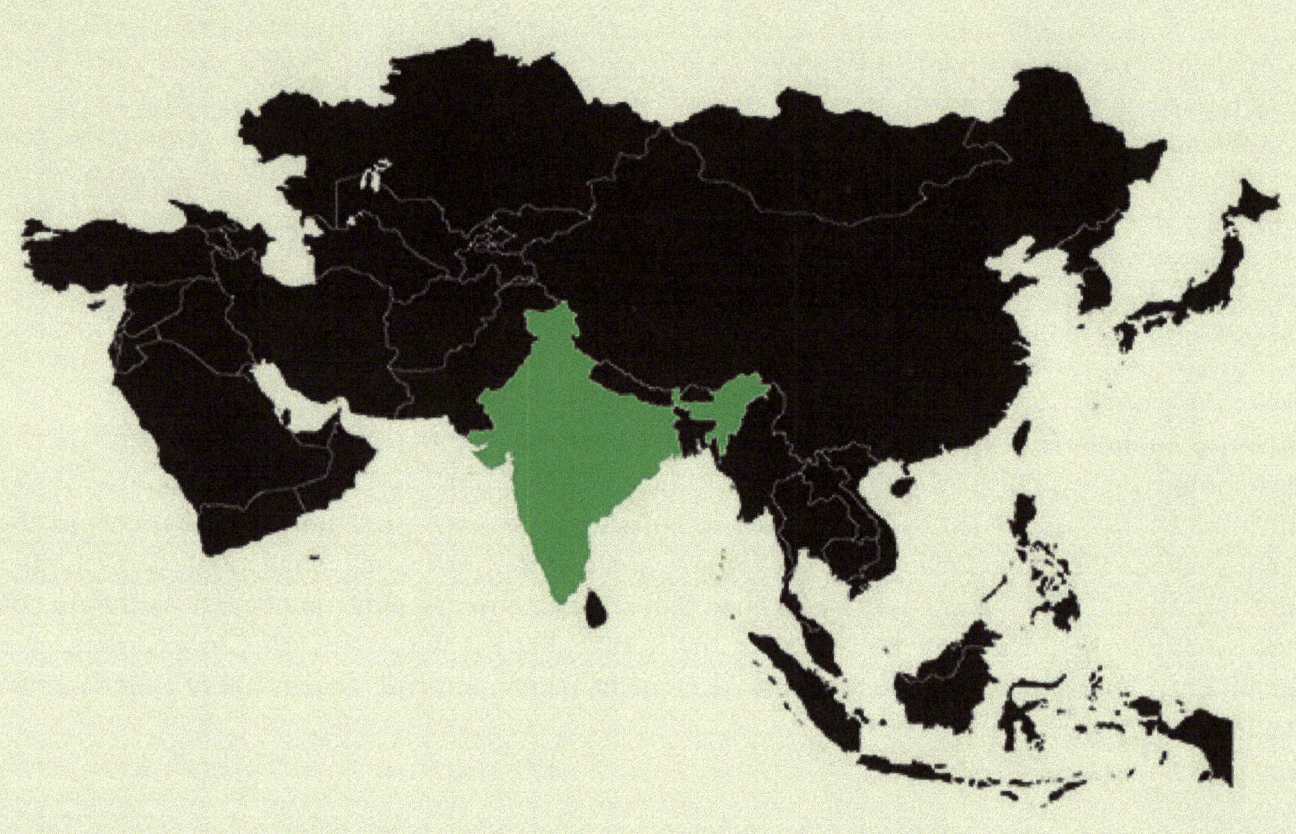

INDIA

India is a vast country located in southern Asia. As with other countries, what they eat there depends upon the region. With over 20 different regions of India there are a lot of different styles of cooking! If there is one thing most regions have in common it's the use of delicious spices. Here are just a few spices to be found in Indian cooking.

Turmeric. A rhizome (underground stem), actually, turmeric is a plant native to India and related to ginger. While fresh turmeric is sometimes used in Indian cooking, more often it is boiled, dried and ground to a deep-yellow powder. Turmeric is an essential ingredient throughout India and gives many dishes a vibrant yellow color and a mellow, warm flavor.

Cumin. Small, elongated, ridged seeds from the Cuminum cyminum plant give dishes a pungent, flavor. The seeds are almost always toasted before being used whole, crushed or ground.

Coriander. The round, tan seeds of the coriander plant (Coriandrum sativum) have an earthy smell and flavor and are used whole, crushed or ground, often in conjunction with cumin.

Mustard Seeds. Brown mustard seeds, also sold as black mustard seeds, are toasted in a dry pan, or tossed in hot oil until they pop, giving them a warm, nutty flavor.

Cardamon. Cardamom, either green (choti elaichi) or brown (badi elchi or moti elaichi). is used in curries, sweet dishes, or in the spice blend, garam masala.

Cinnamon The fragrant, sweet, and spicy rolled and dried inner bark of the Cinnamomum zeylanicum or the cassia tree. Used as a whole stick for infusion or ground as a seasoning to flavor both sweet and savory dishes.

Cauliflower & Pea Curry

Curry is a dish loosely translated as "cooked in liquid." In Indian cuisine, the liquid is often coconut milk, tomato sauce, yogurt, or sometimes all of the above. This curry recipe is considered more "dry" curry. Dry curries are cooked with just a little liquid and the liquid is allowed to evaporate. Wet curries have more sauce and often use coconut milk or cream.

The ingredients for this recipe may not be readily found in most supermarkets. If you can't find mustard or cumin seeds, substitute with powder. Or make your own curry spice blend following the recipe on the following pages.

1 head of cauliflower
1 cup of frozen peas
2 tablespoon vegetable oil
1 teaspoon mustard seeds (or ½ teaspoon powdered mustard)
1 teaspoon cumin seeds (or ½ teaspoon powdered cumin)
½ teaspoon turmeric powder
½ teaspoon red chili powder (optional)
1 teaspoon coriander
1 teaspoon cumin powder
1 cup water
1 handful of fresh coriander or cilantro to garnish

Chop the cauliflower into small cubes. Place the turmeric, chili powder, coriander, and cumin powder into a small bowl and mix together. Put the cumin seeds and mustard seeds into a small bowl. These seeds will need to be added quickly to the oil. Heat the oil in a large saucepan or skillet over a medium flame and make sure the lid is set aside within easy reach (the seeds may pop out from the hot oil when the cauliflower is added so it's good to have the lid nearby to cover up quickly). Test the oil by adding a couple of mustard and cumin seeds. If they sizzle, it's ready. Add the remaining seeds and add the chopped cauliflower and peas and cover. Turn the heat down and then add the remaining spices and stir through with a fork. Pour the water over the mixture, cover, and leave to cook with the lid on until the cauliflower is soft giving the mixture an occasional stir. If it starts to stick, it's too hot so turn the heat down and add a little more water. Garnish with chopped, fresh coriander and serve with plain boiled rice, plain yogurt, and nan bread.

Nan or Naan Bread
(makes 10)

If you go to an Indian restaurant, most likely naan bread will be on the menu. I've been to weddings where the naan bread is made from scratch and cooked in a traditional tandoor oven. It was fun to watch but I know most of us do not have the space for a tandoor oven in our home. If you have a cast iron skillet, you can make nan bread. In our afterschool classes we use an electric skillet. Both work great.

2 cups flour
2 cups natural yogurt (Greek or otherwise)
1 tablespoon baking powder
1 teaspoon sea salt

Place flour, baking powder, yogurt, and salt in a bowl and mix until a dough begins to form and the ingredients come together. Use your hands for this ~ it's fun! Dust a work surface with flour and place dough onto it. Knead for 1 minute to bring all the ingredients together. Divide the dough into 10 equal-sized pieces and using a flour-dusted rolling pin (or your hands), roll into 5-inch circles. Heat a skillet to medium heat (do not use any oil or butter to grease) and cook each flatbread for 2 minutes on each side until puffy and charred. Serve with curry or brush with garlic, oil, or ghee. Enjoy!

Curry Spice Blend

As part of our Spice Skills and Herb Rules class, we will make spice blends, like the curry spice blend below. This is just one way to make a curry spice blend. For almost every house in India, there is a unique spice blend (or many) that may have been handed down from generation to generation. I am a humble person and do not believe for a second this is the "one true" curry blend. But consider it a start.

One thing you must do, if you can. Toast the seeds before grinding to bring out the flavor.

2 tablespoons whole cumin seeds, toasted
2 tablespoons whole cardamom seeds, toasted
2 tablespoons whole coriander seeds, toasted
1/4 cup ground turmeric
1 tablespoon dry mustard
1 teaspoon cayenne

Using a spice grinder or coffee grinder, which you don't mind corrupting with spices, grind seeds and then mix with ground spices in a small bowl. Salt to taste and use to season curries, stews, and roasted and grilled vegetables.

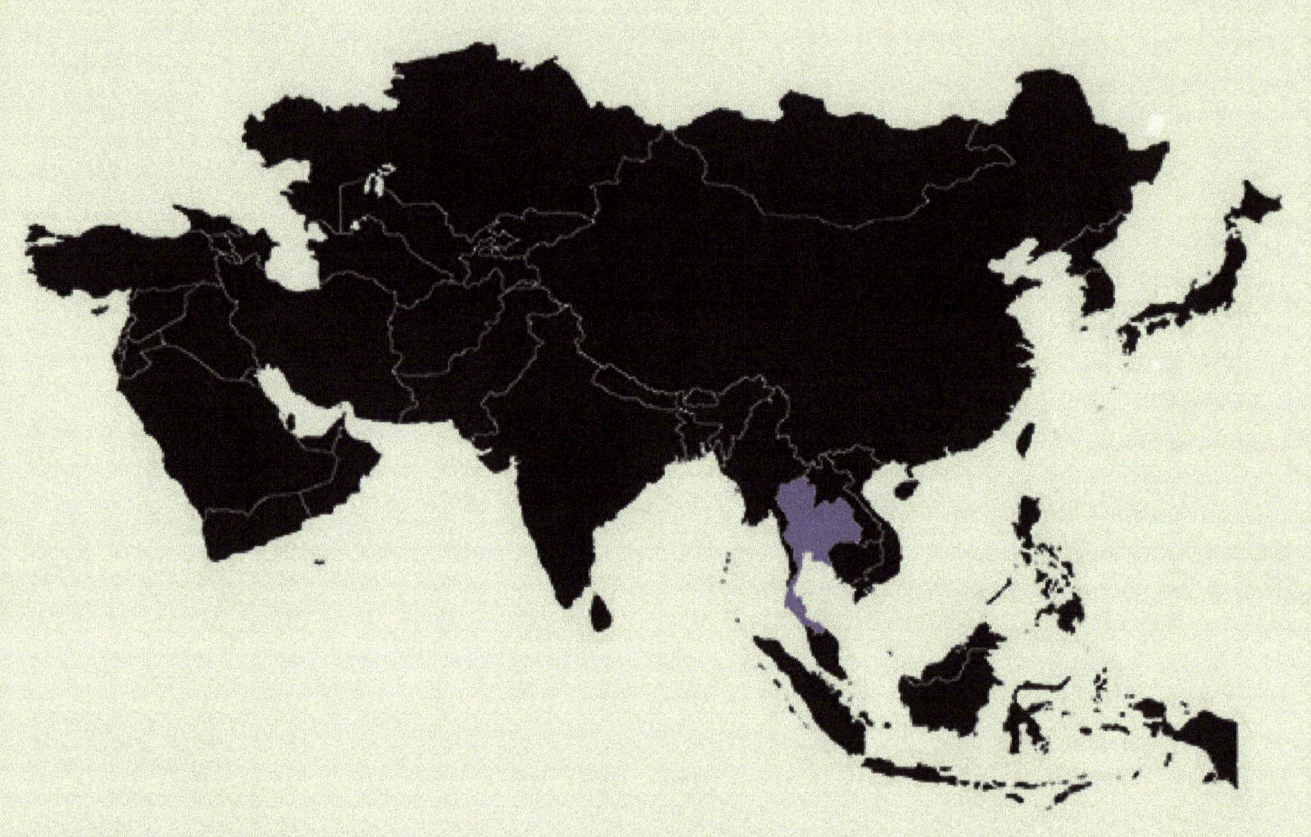

THAILAND

Thailand is located in the center of mainland Asia and has a tropical climate. Unlike other countries in its vicinity, it has never been colonized.

One of the most popular types of Asian style cuisine throughout the world is Thai cuisine. It features lightly prepared dishes with strong aromatic components and a spicy edge. Thai cuisine is sour, sweet, salty, bitter, and spicy, often all at once. In a good way. Australian chef David Thompson said it best:

> "Thai food [is] about the juggling of disparate elements to create a harmonious finish.... Simplicity isn't the dictum here, at all. Some westerners think it's a jumble of flavors, but to a Thai that's important, it's the complexity they delight in.".

Green Papaya Salad (Som Tum)

(Serves 2-6 as part of a meal)

The best papaya salad I had was in the night markets of Chang Rai and Chang Mai, two cities in northern Thailand. They grate the papaya right in front of you and make the dressing on the spot. Not every Thai restaurant in the United States will serve this dish so it's nice to be able to know how to make it at home. It's a delicious and refreshing recipe for the summer, especially when you don't feel like cooking or if it's too hot to cook.

1 medium-sized green papaya
5 cherry tomatoes, cut in half
½ cup long beans, cut into ½-inch pieces
1 clove garlic
2 rounds of palm sugar (or 1 tablespoon of brown sugar)
Juice of 1-2 limes
2-4 tablespoons fish sauce, depending on taste
¼ cup roasted peanuts
1 small Thai chili, deseeded (optional)
Wedge of cabbage, to serve.

Peel and grate papaya. Set aside. Lightly crush garlic in Thai-style mortar and add chili if using (the more you crush the chili, the spicier the salad will be). If not preparing in Thai Style mortar, can mix ingredients in a bowl. If using a mixing bowl, crush garlic by hand and place it in a medium-sized bowl. Grate or crush the palm sugar in a stone mortar or measure brown sugar as a substitute. Add sugar, fish sauce, and lime juice to a Thai-style mortar or bowl. Mix until the sugar is dissolved. Add papaya, mix and toss to combine. Add long beans, and mix. Add tomatoes, and mix. Add peanuts, and lightly mix so as not to crush them too much. Adjust to taste. If it is too sweet, add a splash of fish sauce. If it is too fishy, add some sugar.

Sticky Rice with Mango
(Served as dessert or snack)

I have a strong sweet tooth and one of the things I like most about Thai cuisine are the desserts. Some are simple yet delicious, like this Sticky Rice with Mango.

3 cups short or medium grain rice, soaked overnight in water or thin coconut milk and drained
2 cups canned or fresh coconut milk
3/4 cup palm sugar, or substitute brown sugar
1 teaspoon salt
4 ripe mangoes, or substitute sliced ripe peaches or papayas

Steam the rice until tender. Place the coconut milk in a heavy pot and heat over medium heat until hot. Add the sugar and salt and stir until it is dissolved. When the rice is tender, turn it out into a bowl and pour 1 cup of the hot coconut milk over; reserving the rest. Stir to mix the liquid into the rice, then let stand for 20 minutes to an hour to allow the flavors to blend.

Meanwhile, peel the mangoes. Hold the mango upright and slice lengthwise about 1/2 inch from the center — your knife should cut just along the flat side of the pit. Repeat on the other side of the pit. Lay each mango half flat and slice thinly lengthwise.

To serve individually, place an oval mound of sweetened rice on each dessert plate and place a sliced half-mango decoratively beside it. Top with sesame seeds, if you wish. Or, place the mango slices on a platter and pass it around, together with a serving bowl containing the rice, allowing guests to serve themselves. Stir the remaining sweetened coconut milk thoroughly, transfer it to a small serving bowl or pitcher, and pass it around separately.

AUSTRALIA

Is Australia a continent or a country? It's both, actually. Australia is considered a continent for both historical reasons and also because the Australian continental shelf separates it from the rest of Southeast Asia.

Is it an island? Some say yes, others say no. In other words, it's complicated. Many say it's not an island because its unique flora and fauna (plants and animals, that is) makes it more of a continent. In addition, its indigenous people, the Aborigines, have a separate culture and traditions which makes the land mass more continent than island. As this book is more about cooking than geography, let's agree to reserve the question of whether Australia is a continent or island for a future report or debate club topic.

AUSTRALIA ~ THE COUNTRY

Australia, formally known as the Commonwealth of Australia, is a large land mass surrounded by the Indian and Pacific Oceans. Its history is deep and disturbing, rich and replete with stories and sagas. Starting over 70,000 years ago, the Aboriginal Australians first came to the land. These people learned to live in the harshest of conditions, such as the dry deserts of the interior of Australia and ate what food they could hunt or gather. In 1788 England claimed ownership. Later they used their new colony as a prison, turning it into a colony of convicts. And let's not forget about its flora and fauna. To make things even more intriguing, Australia is home to the world's most deadliest spider, the funnel web spider, and the world's most deadliest snake, the inland tapien.

Wheat, rice, oranges, bananas, and grapes are just a few of the crops that grow in abundance throughout the country. Meat has always been a large part of the Australian diet, although recently Australians are eating healthier fare. Many of the foods Australians consider traditional have interesting histories and stories.

Anzac Biscuits
(makes about 2 to 3 dozen)

IT'S NOT A COOKIE ~ IT'S A BISCUIT

Similar to the English, Australians refer to what those from the United States know as "cookies" as "biscuits." At least that's the proper term. Australians have an amazing way with phrasing and words. Somewhere along the way they took the word "biscuits" and changed it into "bikies" or "bikkies." Remember, if you're visiting Australia and someone asks you over for "tea and bikkies" that's a good thing.

An **Anzac biscuit** is a sweet biscuit, popular in Australia and New Zealand, made using rolled oats, flour, unsweetened coconut flakes, sugar, butter, syrup, baking soda, and hot water. Anzac biscuits were sent to the Australian and New Zealand Army Corps (ANZAC) during World War I as the ingredients did not spoil easily while traveling across the seas. They have a special place in Australia history and food culture. Taste a ANZAC biscuit and taste a little bit of Australian history.

- 1 cup oats (not instant)
- 1 cup flaked coconut (preferably unsweetened)
- ¾ cup flour
- ½ cup sugar
- ½ cup butter
- 1 tablespoon golden syrup (we use maple syrup)
- 2 tablespoons of boiling water
- 1 teaspoon baking soda

Preheat the oven to 325 F. Combine oats, coconut, flour, and sugar. Melt the butter with the syrup. Heat a pan of water on the stove until it boils. Remove from heat. Add the baking soda to 2 tablespoons of the boiling water in a small bowl, then stir into the golden syrup and butter mixture. Create a well in the middle of the dry ingredients.

Pour in the butter and golden syrup mixture. Stir gently to incorporate the dry ingredients.

Using a measuring tablespoon, scoop out a rounded spoonful of dough and then place onto a buttered baking sheet, placing each scoop of dough about 1 inch apart so that the dough has room to spread as they bake. Bake in batches for 8-10 minutes until golden. Transfer to a wire rack to cool.

> **What is golden syrup?**
>
> *Golden syrup, also known as light treacle, is not easily found in the United States, so we use maple syrup in our classes.*

Vegemite Sandwich

Australians are very resourceful and entrepreneurial. The invention of vegemite is a perfect example of such traits. Following the disruption of marmite imports into Australia after World War I, an Australian company by the name of Fred Walker & Co. gave its employee the task of creating a spread from the used yeast dumped by breweries. They took the yeast, concentrated it, and blended it with salt, celery, and onion extracts to form a sticky black paste and called it Vegemite. Considered an Australian staple, it is one of the richest vegetarian sources of B vitamins and folic acid. The traditional way to eat it is on toast with lots of butter and a thin spread of vegemite on top. Most Aussies recommend, "the thinner the layer, the better."

VEGEMITE DARE

Unless you grew up with Vegemite, you might not like the taste. Maybe some Australians don't like it either and that's why they say "the thinner the layer, the better." But I love it! Served with sliced tomatoes, it has a savory, salty flavor and when it's served with the right bread and the right fixings, a Vegemite sandwich is a tasty snack or lunch. Try this recipe and then try it three more times. I hope by the third time you'll be hooked.

One slice of bread
Softened butter
Vegemite
Choose from any or all of the following: sliced tomatoes,
sliced avocado, one lettuce leaf, sliced radishes

Toast bread. With a knife spread butter evenly over toast. With the same knife spread Vegemite thinly over buttered toast. Top with any of the items listed above or all of them. Eat as an open-faced sandwich.

NEW ZEALAND

> New Zealand is technically not part of the Australian continent. Why did we include it under this chapter then? It is located geographically speaking, close to the continent of Australia. I apologize in advance to any NZ citizens if the organization of this book offends you.

New Zealand is a remote group of mountainous islands in the southeastern Pacific Ocean. There are two main islands, North and South, separated by the Cook Strait. The islands were created just 23 million years ago when the land was thrust out of the ocean by volcanic forces. New Zealand has quite a range when it comes to natural landscapes and elements~ volcanoes, some of which are still active today, sharp snowy peaks, rocky shores, and pastures. And let's not forget the waterfalls.

When you visit New Zealand be sure to stop at a waterfall or two, or three or four. I traveled to New Zealand and we rented what is called a "camper van" and traveled the countryside and coastline of the northern and southern islands. On the first day we were driving down the road and I saw a sign for a waterfall. "Pull over!" I yelled at my husband driving the van. We stopped and took so many pictures of the waterfall! We got back in the van and drove further down the road. About 10 kilometers down the road was another sign for a waterfall. "Pull over!" I yelled again. We got out of the van and took more pictures. And so it went for about two more hours and several more waterfalls. We soon learned that New Zealand had a LOT of waterfalls and if we stopped at every one we would not get very far. So when you go to New Zealand, enjoy the scenery but don't forget about your destination.

Pavlova

This dessert – a simple meringue with fruit and cream – was named after the Russian ballerina Anna Pavlova. Ms. Pavlova visited both Australia and New Zealand in the 1920s and this dessert was allegedly created in her honor. The Oxford English Dictionary holds New Zealand to be the place of origin of pavlova, although an Australian may vehemently disagree. Knowing I might make some Australians upset I decided to put this recipe in the New Zealand category. Please don't be too upset with me, Australia.

What differentiates this dessert from a typical meringue is the addition of vinegar and cornstarch (traditional recipes use cornflour). Both help to give the outside a lovely crunchy shell, while the inside remains soft like a marshmallow.

Ingredients
4 egg whites (5 if you are using small eggs)
1 cup (250g) fine castor sugar, sifted
1 teaspoon white vinegar
1 teaspoon cornstarch, sifted
1 teaspoon vanilla

About caster sugar: castor sugar is refined cane sugar, more fine than regular table sugar for sale in most countries. Using regular cane sugar is not an exact substitute for castor sugar but I have found if you sift it a couple of times, you can use regular cane sugar for this recipe.

Preheat your oven to 225 F. Line a baking sheet with parchment paper. Draw a 9 inch circle in the middle of the paper and flip the paper so that you can see the outline of the circle.

Beat the egg whites on a medium setting until soft peaks form. Once soft peaks appear, slowly add the sugar all at once while continuously mixing on full speed. As you are adding the sugar the mixture should become glossy. When the mix reaches the "ribbon" stage, a spoonful of the meringue mixture poured back into the bowl sits on the surface like a ribbon, slow the machine and add the vinegar and vanilla. Turn off the mixer and fold in the cornstarch, folding in no more than four to six rotations. Turn out the mixture onto the sheet pan and mold into a circular shape. Place the tray in the middle of the oven and bake for 1 and ½ hours. Turn off oven and allow meringue to cool in oven with door slightly ajar. After the meringue has cooled pipe or smooth whipped cream atop the meringue and decorate with fresh fruit. Note: if you don't eat the pavlova immediately it will deflate a little, so dive in!

NORTH AMERICA

North America, the third largest continent, is located entirely in the Northern hemisphere. To the north is the Arctic Ocean, the east is the Atlantic and the west is the Pacific. It is on the North American tectonic plate and includes 23 countries, including Greenland. With 23 countries in this continent alone, the food is as diverse as the people who live there. We give tribute to North America with three countries ~ Cuba, Mexico, and the United States of America.

CUBA

Cuba is one large island surrounded by smaller ones in the northern part of the Caribbean Sea, only about 100 miles south of Florida. To understand Cuban cuisine one must first understand a little about its history.

Cuba was originally inhabited by two distinct indigenous peoples: **Taíno and Ciboney** (or Siboney). The first European to visit what we know today as Cuba was Christopher Columbus who in 1492, "claimed" it in the name of Spain. Spain brought more people over to the island and they formed a colony. Their treatment of the native inhabitants was brutal. They forced them into slavery and soon they were nearly extinct. Then the Spanish colonists brought people from Africa and forced them into slavery to work on the plantations and in the mines.

This history is reflected in the foods of modern day Cuban cuisine. Because of Cuba's history of colonization and slavery, many Cuban recipes share spices and techniques with Spanish and African cooking, along with some Caribbean influence.

Moros y Cristianos ~ Black Beans & Rice

Moros y Cristianos is more than a recipe. It is also a history lesson. It translates into "Moors and Christians." The black beans represent the Muslim Moors who battled the Spanish Christians, represented by the white rice, in a long drawn out battle known as the Reconquista. Over time and with a lot of effort at reconciliation, these two groups came to live together in the Iberian Peninsula. You can serve the rice and beans separately and mix on your plate or mix prior to serving. But the intent is to mix.

1 cup long or short grain rice, uncooked
1 15 oz. can of black beans, rinsed and drained
2 tablespoons olive oil
1/2 red onion, peeled and finely chopped
2 cloves garlic, peeled and finely chopped
1/2 teaspoon salt
2 teaspoons fresh or dried oregano
1 teaspoon ground cumin
1 tablespoon red wine vinegar

Cook rice according to the package directions. Meanwhile, heat oil in a saucepan over medium-high heat. Add the onion, garlic, salt and cook, stirring occasionally, until softened, 5 to 7 minutes. Stir in the cumin. Add the beans, oregano, and a little water. Simmer, covered, for 10 minutes. Add the vinegar. Smash some beans with the back of a fork to thicken. Serve over the rice or mix together. Top with radishes or cilantro or avocado and serve with fried plantains.

Fried plantains

Ripe plantains are best. The peels should be almost completely black. A thick bottomed skillet works best for this dish.

2 to 3 blackened plantains
4 tablespoons unsalted butter
1 teaspoon ground cinnamon
1 teaspoon vanilla extract
2 tablespoons brown sugar
Additional butter for topping

Peel plantains, cut off ends, and discard peels. Slice plantains in half lengthwise. Mix cinnamon, vanilla, and sugar together and set aside in a small bowl. Heat butter in a large skillet and place over medium-low heat. Fry the plantains in a single layer until golden on the bottom, then turn over with a spatula. Layer the cinnamon, vanilla, and sugar mix over plantains and let cook a few more seconds, just until the sugar begins to caramelize. Just before serving, melt about 1 tablespoon of butter and drizzle over plantains. Serve immediately with limes, coconut, or sour cream.

MEXICO

Mexico is a country in North America that borders the United States to the north. To its south and west lies the Pacific and just southeast are the countries of Guatemala, Belize, and the Caribbean Sea. East of Mexico is the Gulf of, you guessed it, Mexico! Beaches, mountains, deserts, and jungles are all a part of Mexico.

Much of what we think of as authentic Mexican food may have come from the Mayan Indians, the first people who settled in this area. For example, corn tortillas with bean paste were a common food item of the Mayan people as well as the Aztecs, another tribe who settled in northern Mexico around the beginning of the 13th century.

CORN CURRENCY

Corn is the foundation of the Mexican diet, as it has been for thousands of years. From tortillas to tamales, it can be found in almost every meal. Before the Spanish arrived in what we now know as Mexico, the Aztecs not only grew corn but worshipped it. The Aztecs believed that everything in their world, human and natural, had spiritual power. As they worshiped the earth, the sun, the water, and all foods which grew and gave them life, corn was imbued with special significance and meaning. Corn, or maize, was so important in their culture that they celebrated the different stages of its growth, from seed to sprout to food and back to seed for planting. One could not give tribute to Mexican food culture without first giving tribute to corn.

Homemade Tortillas
(easier than you think!)
(makes 18 to 20 small tortillas)

We use this recipe to make tostadas in class and at home as they fry up crispy or as a side to serve with rice and beans. If you wish to make a tortilla a little softer and flexible for tacos add a little oil to the recipe. To properly make corn tortillas you'll something called **masa harina, a special corn flour.** It also helps to have a tortilla press but with a little practice, you can make them by hand, too.

2 cups masa harina
1 1/3 cup warm water
¼ teaspoon salt

Mix ingredients and let sit for five minutes. Then begin working the masa mix with your hands to make the dough, kneading it for several minutes to make sure all the ingredients are thoroughly combined. Take a golf-ball-sized piece of dough and shape it into a ball. Repeat to make 16 to 18 balls.

If you are using a tortilla press use a plastic bag in the shape of the tortilla press. Open the press and place on a piece of plastic on the bottom center of the press. Place a masa ball between the plastic pieces. Gently close the press and press down, until the dough has spread out about six inches. If you don't have a tortilla press simply take a ball and smash it between the palms of your two hands, then keep pressing the dough into the shape of a tortilla which should be about 1/8 to ¼ inch thick and about a 6-inch wide circle. Do this for all 16 to 18 balls and you'll either wish you had a tortilla press or you will feel like an expert tortilla maker.

Heat a griddle or a large skillet on high heat. One at a time, gently lay the tortilla down on the skillet. Cook the tortilla on the hot pan for 30 seconds to a minute on each side. The tortilla should be lightly toasted. Little air pockets may start forming. Remove the tortillas and wrap them in a dish towel to keep them warm. Serve immediately or refrigerate and reheat.

Tostadas

The tradition of tostadas dates back about 2,000 years and is said to be invented in Oaxaca, Mexico. Tostadas became a delicious and hearty way to extend and make use of leftover tortillas that were no longer fresh enough to fold for tacos but still fresh enough to be eaten.

In class, we make our tostada shells fresh using the recipe for tortillas in this book. We then lightly fry the tortillas in vegetable oil and sprinkle a little salt on top. It makes Tostada Tuesday all the more special!

- 1 can of pinto beans, opened but not drained
- 2 tablespoons oil
- 1 teaspoon of cumin
- 2 teaspoons mild ground chili powder
- 6 to 8 tostada shells
- 1 cabbage or head of lettuce
- 1 bottle of vinegar (white, red wine, or apple cider)
- 2 small or 1 large, ripe avocado
- 1 bunch cilantro
- 1 to 2 limes
- Salt and pepper
- 1 bottle of oil, vegetable or canola
- 1 cup bottled or fresh salsa (more to taste)
- 1 package of queso fresco or shredded cheese
- optional: sour cream

Drain off about 1/2 cup of liquid from the beans, retaining it in a separate bowl to use later for moistening the beans, should they dry out. Heat oil over medium-high heat in a large, heavy nonstick frying pan and add ground cumin and chili. Cook, stirring over medium heat, for about a minute, until the spices begin to sizzle and cook. Add beans and cook at a brisk simmer, stirring and mashing with the back of your spoon, a potato masher or a wooden pestle, until they thicken and begin to get crusty on the bottom. Stir up the crust each time it forms, and mix it into the beans. Cook until beans are thick but not dry, 10 to 15 minutes. They will continue to thicken and dry out when you remove them from the heat. Add liquid you saved from the beans if they seem too dry, but save some of the liquid for moistening the beans if you are serving them later. Taste and adjust salt (they probably won't need any as the broth reduces when you refry them).

Shred cabbage and sprinkle a little vinegar and oil and salt and pepper on cabbage to season. Set aside.

Spread a layer of refried beans (about 2 tablespoons) over each tostada shell. Top with cabbage. Spoon salsa over the cabbage and top with sliced or diced avocado, a sprinkling of chopped cilantro and a sprinkling of queso fresco or yellow grated cheese. Serve.

UNITED STATES OF AMERICA

Fifty states covering a vast expanse of land called the United States of America. This is the country where I say am from when I travel internationally. Yet I know next to nothing about Montana, or what they cook there, and the same is true for Oklahoma or Maryland. I've tried to teach a class series exploring the cuisine of the United States and I learned it there is much to discover and appreciate about all the states and how each one has its own culture and identity. I love that this country is as diverse as the food culture in other expansive countries such as China. To pay homage to my home country I looked back to childhood experiences ~ a vacation to the Florida Keys and my time as Girl Scout.

Key Lime Pie

It was on a trip to visit my brother in Florida in the 1970's that my mother and I first discovered key lime pie. As we strolled the boardwalk in Pompano Beach postcards had a recipe for key lime pie on it. We grabbed as many recipe postcards as we could and scoured the local markets for key lime juice to take back as souvenirs. At home we tested out the recipe from the postcard and shared our newly found pie with friends and family. It's sweet, it's sour, and it is beautiful to behold. It's also even better if you let it sit overnight in the refrigerator.

About key limes: key limes get their name from the Florida keys but are now grown in other parts of the country, including California. They are smaller than the limes you will see in the market, which are generally Persian limes. They are a little more fragile than the market limes and are said to have a more floral bouquet than Persian limes. If you can't find key limes, try either buying bottled key lime juice or the market limes. Or do your own taste test to see if you notice a difference.

Crust
14 graham crackers (about 1½ sleeves)
4-6 tablespoons unsalted butter, melted
1 tablespoon sugar
½ teaspoon kosher salt

Filling
3 egg yolks
1 14-ounce can of sweetened condensed milk
2 teaspoons finely grated lime zest, plus more for garnish
⅔ cup fresh key lime (or regular lime) juice
Pinch of kosher salt

For the crust

Preheat the oven to 325°. Using food processor, pulse crackers until coarsely ground. The texture should be like sand. Pour into bowl and mix with butter, sugar, and salt and mix until well blended. Add to a 9" pie dish and press mix evenly into the bottom and up sides of the dish. Bake crust until golden brown on top and crumbs are set, 12-15 minutes. Let cool.

For the Filling
Using an electric mixer on medium speed or whisk, beat egg yolks and condensed milk in a large bowl until paler and almost doubled in volume, about 5 minutes. Whisk lime zest, lime juice, and salt into mixture. Pour into the cooled crust. Bake pie until filling is set (it should not be jiggly and will be slightly puffy at the edges), about 15-20 minutes. Let cool completely. Garnish with whipped cream and lime zest.

S'mores

I was a Girl Scout from a young child until my last day of high school. As an adult I was a Girl Scout leader for over seven years. I've never been on a Girl Scout camping trip without s'mores. And for good reason.

S'mores are a melty, toasty marshmallow paired with a piece of chocolate. You mash the toasted marshmallow and chocolate between two graham crackers and devour them.

The Girl Scouts of America recorded the first "recipe" in their 1927 guidebook. The name comes from the phrase "gimme some more." The tasty treat is still popular around campfires across the country. While you don't have to be a Girl Scout to make them, I would consider it. Better yet, consider donating to the Girl Scouts of America in honor of s'mores.

Until this book, I've never written a recipe for s'mores. We just made them over open flames while camping as a family or with the Girl Scouts. Once you make them, you won't need to refer back to the recipe.

Large marshmallows
Chocolate bars
Graham crackers
Metal skewers or wood skewes (wood skewers should be soaked in water for at least 20 minutes to prevent catching fire)

Skewer marshmallows and over an open flame or grill, toast marshmallows, rotating them, unti they are softened and the outside appears browned. You can also char them if you like the taste of burnt marshmallows. It. Place on the edge of the grill just until the chocolate is warmed and softened, about 30 seconds. until the marshmallow puffs and turns golden brown, 1 to 2 minutes. Remove marshmallow from skewer by squishing the marshmallow between two graham cracker squares with a bar of milk chocolate on the bottom. You can also top the marshmallow with the chocolate and then add the top graham cracker square. Eat while everthing is warm and gooey.

SOUTH AMERICA

Above South America, to the northwest and north is the is the Caribbean Sea. The Atlantic Ocean lies to the northeast, east, and southeast, and the Pacific Ocean to the west. In the northwest it is joined to North America by the Isthmus of Panama, a land bridge narrowing to about 50 miles (80 km) at one point. Drake Passage, south of Cape Horn, separates South America from Antarctica. Geographically, the continent contains an amazing natural wonders, including some of the largest waterfalls, longest rivers, glaciers, mountains, and more. If you haven't been there yet, I suggest that you go. In the meantime, check out some recipes from Brazil, Argentina, and Peru.

BRAZIL

Look at a map of South America and you will see that Brazil represents half of the continent. It is also the 5th largest country in the world. It is unique in South America in that the official language is not Spanish but Porteguese. Of the ten countries which speak Porteguese, Brazil is the largest. This means that there are more people speaking Porteguese in Brazil than in Portugal. The world can be a very fascinating place.

Brazil surprised me greatly in terms of food culture. I marveled at the fact that they had so much kale on the menu, an influence from their colonialization by the Porteguese. I love kale and I was always impressed by how they served it, everything from soups to sides and more. While most restaurants focus on the carne, or meats, of Brazil, if I were to open a Brazilan restaurant I would make it all about the kale. We have a few delicious Brazilian recipes which feature kale on our website worthy of your next weekly meal plan.

As much as I like to introduce healthy greens to the masses, I confess that in our children's cooking classes we focus on the sweet treats. We love to celebrate Brazil with brigaideiros. Rich in both flavor and history, the ingredients are simple and the technique does need some finessing but you an master it with a little practice.

Brigadeiro

BRIGADEIRO is a bite-sized Brazilian chocolate sweet. Brigadeiro is the word in Portuguese for brigadier, a lower ranking general. This little chocolate treat was named after the Brazilian Brigadier, Eduardo Gomes, who in 1945 started his presidential campaign. Possessing good looks and known for his charming speeches, female fans flocked to his side. These entrepreneurial women then created candies and sold them to raise funds for his campaign. At that time, campaign parties were in vogue and soon people were calling friends to attend Gomes' parties and to try the sweets. Even though it was the women supporting Gomes who made them, the candy's name soon morphed into "Brigadeiro."

3 tablespoons unsweetened cocoa powder
1 can sweetened condensed milk
1 tablespoon butter

In a medium saucepan mix cocoa, butter and condensed milk over medium heat. Cook, stirring, until thickened, about 10 minutes. Remove from heat and let rest until cool enough to handle. Form into small balls and eat at once or chill until serving.

> Don't stop stirring!! What most recipes fail to tell you is as the three ingredients are cooking you need to stir and stir and stir while scraping the bottom and sides of the saucepan. The mixture will thicken and begin to pull away from the sides. When it does this your brigadeiros are done and can be cooled.

ARGENTINA

Shaped like a wedge on the western side of South America Argentina lies in the southern hemisphere. Because of this, Argentina's winter months are May through August and it's hottest in January. Similar to the United States, the country is made of many immigrants, the earliest of which were from Italy and Spain. Both the Italians and the Spaniards brought their culture and food which produced an Argentinian type of cuisine combining pizza, pasta, and their most famous item ~ empanadas.

While traveling throughout Argentina I couldn't eat enough empanadas. I took a cooking class on how to make them and even won the contest for making the best empanada! Besides empanadas, Argentinian cuisine has an amazing fusion of Italian and South American influences and you can find the Italian influences throughout the country. For example, in the middle of the remote regions of Patagonia, I could order risotto (an Italian rice dish).

My favorite dessert was the national cookie called alfajores. While I did not have a chance to learn how to make them in Argentina I definitely ate enough of them to want to try to make them back home. In one of our cooking camps we tried to make them and succeeded beautifully.

Empanadas

The name comes from the Spanish word "empanar" meaning to wrap in bread. Argentinian empanadas are a common dish served at parties, as a starter, or even as a dessert as they can be filled with items both savory and sweet. Argentinian empanadas, in particular, are considered to be some of the best in the world. This is due to the fact there is so much variation in Argentinian empanada recipes and cooking styles between the different regions of the country.

What you fill your empanada with is really up to you. If you are going to make a savory empanada we suggest making the chimichurri recipe as a dipping sauce. Chimichurri is a green sauce traditionally used for grilled meat but we think it goes great with empanadas.

The Filling
1 cup mashed potatoes
2 cups cauliflower roasted pieces
1-2 tablespoons olive oil
Kosher salt
1/2 cup grated cheese

The Dough
3 cups all-purpose flour
¼ teaspoon salt
6 ounces unsalted butter (1 ½ stick), chilled, and cut into 12 pieces
1 egg
4-5 tablespoons of water

Mix all ingredients together and set aside.

<u>Using food processor:</u>
Mix the flour and salt in a food processor. Add the butter, egg, and water until a clumpy dough forms.

<u>By hand:</u>
Follow the same instruction but use your hands to mix the ingredients together.

It helps to wrap and chill the dough for about 1 hour or more. Take it out of the refrigerator and divide the dough into several small large golf-ball sized balls. Flatten each ball and roll out the dough to a thickness of ¼ of an inch. Cut out round discs using a cookie cutter. To assemble, place a spoonful of the filling on the middle of each disc. Try not to ovestuff them so that they can be sealed properly. To seal, fold one side over and seal the edges with some egg whites. Press down on the edges with the tines of a fork to seal. Brush empanadas with an egg wash.

Bake the empanadas in a pre-heated oven at 375F-400F. Baking time varies based upon the oven and the size of the empanadas, generally about 18-25 minutes – the empanadas will be ready once they are golden.

CHIMICHURRI

½ cup olive oil
1/3 cup fresh parsley, minced
1 clove garlic, minced
1 teaspoon dried oregano
1 teaspoon red wine vinegar
salt and pepper, to taste

Combine all ingredients in a bowl. Let it sit for about 1 to 2 hours. Serve with empanadas.

Alfajores

Alfajores came a long way to get to Argentina. It is said they originated in the Middle East, came to Spain (via the Moors), and then the Spainards brought them in their migrations to Argentina. While a variety of versions can be found in Argentina, their popularity has not migrated north to my country, the United States. So it gave me great pleasure to introduce them to the children in our cooking camps. Making them in class allowed students to work on their precision in cutting out the cookie biscuits. As the biscuits are delicate, they needed to hold them with care while adding the dulce de leche. Making these cookies is an exercise in concentration and focus with a sweet reward at the end.

1 cup all-purpose flour
1 cup cornstarch
1 teaspoon baking powder
¼ teaspoon baking soda
¼ teaspoon kosher salt
½ cup granulated sugar
8 tablespoons unsalted butter (1 stick) at room temperature

2 large egg yolks
2 teaspoon finely grated lemon zest divided.
1 teaspoons vanilla extract
2 tablespoons warm water
1 cup coconut flakes
8 ounces Dulce De Leche homemade or store-bought

Sift together the flour, cornstarch, baking powder, baking soda and kosher salt into a medium bowl. Set aside. In a separate larger bowl, beat sugar and butter until light and fluffy, about 3 minutes. Add yolks, then vanilla, water and lemon zest. Add flour mixture to the wet ingredients, and mix on low speed until the dough just comes together. Wrap the dough in plastic and chill until firm, at least 2 hours.

Heat oven 350 degrees. Line baking sheets with parchment paper. Remove dough from plastic wrap and place on a lightly floured surface, flour a rolling pin and roll out to about ¼ inch thick. Cut the dough with a 2 inch cookie cutter (or you can use a drinking glass with the same measurements). Place cookies on prepared sheet pans about 1 inch apart.

Bake for about 9 minutes or until firm and edges are pale golden and the middle of the cookie is firm. Transfer the baking pan to a rack and allow to cool completely before removing from the baking sheet.

Spread about 1 tablespoon of dulce de leche onto the back of half the cookies. Place a second cookie on top and gently press to create a sandwich and repeat. Roll sides in coconut and dust generously with powdered sugar before serving.

DULCE DE LECHE

Making dulce de leche, a sticky sweet caramelized milk, can be a time consuming and arduous process. Companies sell it in cans for the convenience of home cooks throughout Latin America. If you can find it in your local stores, feel free to use it. Or you can try this method we found online whereby you slow cook a unopened can of sweetened condensed milk for about 2 ½ hours. This process also takes time but you can do other things while the can is cooking on the stove. Just don't leave it unattended.

Directions
Remove the paper label for a can of sweetened condensed milk. Put the can into a medium saucepan and cover it completely with water. Turn the stove to a medium to hig heat. When it starts to boil, lower the heat to a simmer (low to medium) so that water forms tiny bubbles on the bottom of the pan. Cover with a lid. Cook the can for about 2 ½ hours. Check the pot periodically to make sure the water levels are still above the can. If it falls below the top of the can, add more water. After 2 ½ hours, remove from heat and allow can to cool completely.

PERU

Peru is the third largest country in South America, after Brazil and Argentina. Most people live along the coast of the Pacific Ocean, where the capital, Lima, is located.

The national dish of Peru is ceviche. While most people consider ceviche to be a Mexican dish, ceviche is actually said to have originated in Peru about 2,000 years ago and today has its own holiday.

Peruvian ceviche is different from its Mexican counterpart in that it is seabass or sole that is the subject of the denaturing process. In Mexico, most ceviche is made from shrimp and is often served in a tomato-like soup base.

In any ceviche, the seafood is "cooked" using citric acid such as lime, lemon, or even orange juice. This process is called denaturing, which is the changing of the structure of the protein using citric acid instead of the more conventional source of heat, via fire.

Ceviche takes time as the seafood needs to marinate in the citric acid long enough for the protein to denature. In class, we usually do not have the luxury of time so we opt for a more vegetarian approach or we will poach the fish. I realize poaching the fish is not as authentic so my apologies to the Peruvians or any ceviche chefs out there. If you have the time, I suggest trying the traditional approach.

Traditional Peruvian Ceviche

1 ½ pound very fresh and high-quality fish filets, such as halibut or mahi-mahi
1 red onion thinly sliced or diced
10 limes
1–2 habanero peppers, one finely diced and another sliced crosswise
¼ cup fresh cilantro
Salt to taste

Garnish and serving items: lime slices, boiled or steamed sweet potatoes cut into slices lengthwise, plantain chips

Cut the fish into small cubes, place in a glass or ceramic bowl. Add sliced onions, peppers, and juice from limes over the ingredients. Cover and refrigerate for 1 hour. Mix in cilantro and sliced peppers and salt to taste. Serve with garnishes sweet potatoes and plaintain chips.

Veggie Ceviche

As we like to make our classes as inclusive as possible, we strive to include vegetarian recipes as much as possible. This recipe is not the "traditional" ceviche but is a great way to welcome vegetarians and vegans to your table.

1 14-ounce can of garbanzo beans, drained and rinsed
1/2 red onion, diced
1 to 2 plum tomatoes, deseeded and diced
1 to 2 tablespoons chopped cilantro
½ cup freshly squeezed lime (or lemon) juice
1 habanero or jalapeno pepper, seeded and finely sliced
1 avocado
1/4 tsp salt
Tostada shells

Coarsely chop garbanzo beans and place them in a glass or ceramic bowl. Add the lime or lemon juice, tomatoes, red onion, pepper, cilantro, and salt, and toss to combine. Cover and refrigerate for at least 1 hour or up to 4 hours. Just before serving, dice the avocado, add to the ceviche, and gently toss to combine. Serve atop tostada shells or tortilla chips, if desired.

ANTARCTICA

There's one continent left, Antarctica. There are virtually no people on it, except for scientists. In fact, there are no countries on this continent at all. Via an international treaty signed in 1959 it is a continent dedicated to peace and science. It's also the coldest, the driest, and least populated continent on the planet. Given these facts, what would you eat there? This was the question posed to me by Lucas, one of our first students in our Pots, Pans, and Passports class. He challenged me, saying we hadn't covered *all* the continents. I challenged him back. I told him that if he found a recipe based around this continent I promised we would make it in class. The following week he proudly walked into class with a recipe for sledging biscuits.

Sledging Biscuits

This fabled Antarctic food is not something you would choose to eat if there are any alternatives to be found. It is bland and dry. The advantage of the sledging biscuit is that it is compact, physically resilient, high in energy, and stays edible for a long, long time.
It is a simple hard biscuit that can be spread with butter and any other available toppings such as marmite, cheese, etc.

Historically, explorers to this land had sledging biscuits as a part of their staple diet. It's great when you are away from the base and you begin to get hungry from the strenuous activity in the cold, open air of Antarctica. Suddenly, sledging biscuits are almost, nearly delicious.

150 grams flour
½ teaspoon baking soda
½ teaspoon salt
30 grams butter
50 ml cold water

ACKNOWLEDGMENTS

Each time I did a cooking demonstration I would be asked if I had a cookbook for sale. I would stumble and stammer with my words explaining I had big plans and hopes and dreams but presently, nothing in hardcover to give to them. Those days are gone, thanks to the following people.

My undying gratitude and love to my husband, Paul. He is my best friend and co-conspirator in so many projects, including this one. His photography, creative input, and willingness to join me on travel adventures, near and far, make me a very lucky person. I love you, Pablo.

To my mom, to whom I dedicate this book, is the source of it all. She is no longer with us but if she was, I like to think she would be impressed on how I took a family tradition and turned it into cooking class series, a cookbook, and more. Thanks, Mom, wherever you are.

To Selah, who turned up just at the right moment to be here when the cooking, the photography, and the summer heat arrived in full force. You say you are from Hawaii but I think you were sent from heaven. Your artistic input was valuable and very much appreciated.

To all the children and parents of the children, from Mt. Washington to La Canada to The Chandler School, who support Radical Cooks. I am grateful for every day I can teach someone to cook and to be curious about food, culture, and countries around the world.

Let's not forget the school support staff, from the afterschool coordinators like Ms. Brown to the custodians who help me clean up after a class. A cliche though it may be, but it really does take a village.

I thank you all very much.

RESOURCES

I am not an expert on geography. Any references to facts on oceans, seas, land masses, countries, and continents comes from sources such as National Geographic or Brittanica. These are resources I suggest my younger students start with when researching a country or continent. We also spend a lot of time looking at globes and atlases. I love globes and highly recommend them as a staple in your household.

We also have an extensive list of cooking resources and pantry notes and links to order specialty items on our website at www.potspansandpassports.com.

If you wish to make your weekly meal plan a more international one, wa have ideas and suggestions for you at our website.

COOKING CONVERSION CHART

Cooking Measurement Chart

Weight

imperial	metric
1/2 oz	15 g
1 oz	29 g
2 oz	57 g
3 oz	85 g
4 oz	113 g
5 oz	141 g
6 oz	170 g
8 oz	227 g
10 oz	283 g
12 oz	340 g
13 oz	369 g
14 oz	397 g
15 oz	425 g
1 lb	453 g

Measurement

cup	onces	milliliters	tbsp.
8 cup	64 oz	1895 ml	128
6 cup	48 oz	1420 ml	96
5 cup	40 oz	1180 ml	80
4 cup	32 oz	960 ml	64
2 cup	16 oz	480 ml	32
1 cup	8 oz	240 ml	16
3/4 cup	6 oz	177 ml	12
2/3 cup	5 oz	158 ml	11
1/2 cup	4 oz	118 ml	8
3/8 cup	3 oz	90 ml	6
1/3 cup	2.5 oz	79 ml	5.5
1/4 cup	2 oz	59 ml	4
1/8 cup	1 oz	30 ml	3
1/16 cup	1/2 oz	15 ml	1

Temperature

fahrenheit	celsius
100 °F	37 °C
150 °F	65 °C
200 °F	93 °C
250 °F	121 °C
300 °F	150 °C
325 °F	160 °C
350 °F	180 °C
375 °F	190 °C
400 °F	200 °C
425 °F	220 °C
450 °F	230 °C
500 °F	260 °C
525 °F	274 °C
550 °F	288 °C

ABOUT THE AUTHOR

NIna Zippay is a maverick in spirit and in profession. She is currently a writer, chef, and teacher, and has had professional past lives as a lawyer, producer, and, once upon a time, an art gallery manager.

Travel has always been one of her main passions. To meet different people, be it in Bakersfield or Brazil, and appreciate their culture and food is what she loves most about the adventures of the road. When she can't be on the road she keeps her mind stimulated and her family fed trying out new dishes from other countries in her own kitchen where she also hosts her virtual cooking classes.

If she's not cooking or traveling or both, you'll find her spending time outdoors or relaxing with her adorable black pugs, Otto and Noodles.

www.ingramcontent.com/pod-product-compliance
Lightning Source LLC
Chambersburg PA
CBHW062023050526
44107CB00106B/1011